When the Wheels of Fascism Run

A Brief Account of the Rise and Fall of RSS in Kerala

when the wheels of fascism run
a brief account of the rise and fall of rss in kerala

•

p jayarajan

•

first edition
march 2012

•

typesetting and published
chintha publishers, thiruvananthapuram

•

printed
akshara offset, thiruvananthapuram

•

cover
vinod

Distribution

DESHABHIMANI BOOKHOUSE
H O Thiruvananthapuram 695035
Email: chinthapublishers@gmail.com
Website: www.chinthapublishers.com

Branch

Head Office Kunnukuzhi • Overbridge Thiruvananthapuram • KSRTC Bus Station Alappuzha • KSRTC Bus Station Ernakulam • Machingal Lane Thrissur • IG Road Kozhikode • Mavoor Road Kozhikode • NGO Union Building Kannur • Central Bus Terminal Complex Thavakkara Kannur

CR - 1723 / 2885

When the Wheels of Fascism Run

A Brief Account of the Rise and Fall of RSS in Kerala

P Jayarajan

CHINTHA PUBLISHERS
Thiruvananthapuram 695 035
Price: ` 120

Content

Publishers Note

It is a matter of great privilege for Chintha Publishers on presenting before our readers the English version of Sanghar-shangakude Rashtreeyam authored by Comrade P Jayarajan. The book is an astonishing account of the heart-breaking experiences of the author.

Fascism is an ideology based on violation of all fundamental rights of entire society especially minorities, dalits, tribals and women. It has its own philosophy which takes different forms and adopts different methods in different countries and contexts but the philosophy remains the same. M N Roy, one of the founders of Indian Communist Movement was the first to point out the fact that the roots of fascism lie in the Brahmincal religion.

The demolition of Babri Masjid and the man slaughters of the Muslims were the naked forms of Hindutva fascism. Goebbels, Hitler's propagandist wrote, 'The state must have the power to break its own laws.' That was precisely exemplified on 6 December, 1992 in the demolition of Babri Masjid. The ideological offensive and physical violence are predominant components of Hindutva strategy. Presently, the Hindutva ideological hegemony succeeded penetrating even in the minds of some leftists to alter them as soft Hindutvas. It is the process of the communal unconscious which withholds the creative politics of communists based on the strong solidarity with dalits, minorities and marginalized groups.

The massive reception experienced by the 'Sangharshangakude Rashtreeyam' and the lack of adequate publications projecting real political trends in Kerala before the people of the rest of India, prompted the author to bring it out in English.

The Chintha Publishers is proud of bringing out such a popular piece of work on 'real politiq' in English. We hope that it will be well received by the readers.

Chintha Publishers

Preface

I would like to state at the outset that I fell in the idea of writing this book through the roof. Basically I am not an author. I like always to be a humble servant of my people and a faithful comrade of the Communist Party. I might not have gone to the venture to write this book if I had not been attacked by RSS goons that took my life to a coma. My return to life is still a miracle to my people and for me; this is a new chance to serve the people with more dedication. At last that idea is accomplished and my work originally written in Malayalam was received by the people of Kerala enthusiastically. The Malayalam version of this book is running to its fourth edition.

We, the people of Kerala, know a lot about India on very many topics through the translation of important works of eminent authors in other languages. I doubt whether the people of other states know Kerala as we know them through books. We know a lot about the activities of RSS in other states such as UP, Gujarat and in our nearby Karnataka. But the activities of RSS in Kerala as a rear force to launch their terrorist activities are really very little known to Indian readers in other states. This is precisely the reason that made me and my comrades to bring out an English version of my Malayalam book.

It was in the year 1949 a small group of Hindu fundamentalists sneaked into the Babri Masjid in a night to install an idol of Lord Rama there. On the subsequent day of that unfortunate night Jawaharlal Nehru the then Prime Minister of India was informed about the incident that could provoke the secular textural quality of our constitution. He immediately ordered the local administration to take the idol from the Mosque and let it in the river Sarayu. Jawaharlal Nehru was boldly reminding us that the end of Rama was a 'Samadhi' in the river Sarayu as stated in the great classic Ramayana by Valmeeki. But Rama never ended there. Instead, the Sangh Pariwar reincarnated him as a political card to win the elections four decades later.

Nehru belonged to the radical section of the early leaders of the Indian National Congress who were ardent nationalists and anti-communalists. He was right to tell that communalism under the garb of nationalism is the most dangerous political theory which is not easily recognizable by the freedom fighters. While proclaiming this view Nehru was demarcating himself from the Hindu revivalists who considered that Hinduism is India's nationalism. RSS belonged to this genre of nationalism. Even though Nehru could realize the threat posed by Hindu revivalists, the Congress leadership of our time are not serious enough to understand it. Hence congress party had betrayed the spirit of both Gandhiji and Nehru.

As the contemporary Indian politics teaches us that Congress is unable to face the imminent threat of communal nationalism posed by RSS, BJP and Sangh Pariwar, the recent elections in the states of Gujarat, Himachal Pradesh and Karnataka once again expose the inability of Congress to rally all secular and democratic forces against the revivalists. Only in those states where the left parties or other regional parties are dominant, the BJP is rooted out in elections. The history of recent period has proved that the Congress as a party is unable to cope with the necessary ideological weapons to fight out revivalism which is the prime menace to our independence. In Kerala too, the attitude of the

Congress party is very much similar to the national leadership. Whenever the RSS and the Sangh Pariwar are posing a real threat to democracy and communal harmony of the state the left and other democratic forces alone dare to fight it out. The Congress in the days of test is either an onlooker or a silent supporter of the Sangh Pariwar for their petty electoral gains. In that sense the national political scenario is to be dark and gloomy. But fortunately enough it is not totally dark as the glimpses of consistent resistance of the left and other democratic forces are still there in the Indian political horizon.

When election is due in Kerala BJP used to talk high about their influence and always hope to open their account in the legislative assembly. They had played all possible dirty games to win an Assembly seat in the state. BJP leadership in the state know that only by entering in an unholy and hidden truce with the Congress they can materialize their long cherished and long defeated dream. Many a time the Congress was ready to appease the Sangh Pariwar for the sake of popularity. Thus the Congress leaders of Kerala are repeatedly proving themselves that they are not the true followers of both Gandhi and Nehru.

This book is the product of a humble communist trying to remind the readers in other states the real menace posed by the RSS and Sangh Pariwar in the contemporary Indian politics. The activities of the Sangh Pariwar in Kerala are totally different, compared to their activities in northern states. Time and again the RSS leadership had adopted new methods to infiltrate into the masses of Kerala. When one method is defeated they will immediately introduce another one to realize their sole aim of winning a single seat in the Assembly. Their repeated defeats in all attempts to gain a single seat in Kerala Assembly show the finer quality of democracy, secularism and social awareness of the Keralites. In this book I am trying to reveal how the left and democratic forces in Kerala have repeatedly played a positive role to amputate the desire of the RSS and Sangh Pariwar.

Testimony of a Victim

The Onam day that fell on August 25th 1999 is ever memorable to me with a lot of horrible dreams. On the evening of that day I was ruthlessly attacked by RSS miscreants right down at my house where my wife and I Yamuna were alone.

My sons Jain and Ashish were away at Calicut. It was not that much easy to take leave from my hectic political schedule as the election to Parliament was imminent. I was the Secretary of the Election Committee of the parliament constituency of Vadakara.

As the entire state was in a mood of celebration there were no frequent phone calls too. In the evening around 5'O clock while I was sitting in the drawing room of my house I heard a big sound of an explosion close to my house. As I rushed to the front door of my house to see what is happening there took place a second explosion, this time closer. Just after that I heard a scream of a woman just in front of my house. We opened the door and walked out of the house to see what is happening around.

We saw a group of people carrying country made swords and axes and some of them are exploding bombs to create an air of terror. They were all known RSS people. I could easily feel that I am the target and immediately we got into the house and tried to shut the front door. That attempt was in vain as they were large in numbers. They could push it open and get into the room.

They were all shouting slogans *Om Kali Bhadrakali* to reinforce their vigor. Immediately they started their action aiming at me. I could still remember the hauling sound of flashing swords around me. Soon I became wet with blood all over my body. Still I remember that I made an attempt to shield me with a cane chair. But the attack was so rampant that in one dreaded movement my right arm was cut to hang so that I could not carry the shield. I fell down slipping on the pool of blood in my drawing room. Though I tried to get up once again I slipped and fell down. My body was totally numb that I could not move. The RSS goons looked at me for some more moments to confirm my death. After that they returned, throwing country bombs one after another.

Astonishingly enough I was not totally unconscious that I could still feel the thick smoke smelling sulfur coming out of the bombs. My right hand was almost cut out. I could not make an attempt to get up. All these dreaded incidents took place within moments and immediately my neighbors ran to my house to save me. Yamuna, my wife made a call to the party centre at Koothuparamba and they rushed to my house with a vehicle and took me to the Co-operative Hospital, Thalasseri which is about ten kilometers away from my house. Though I was not unconscious then I could not open my eyes because of the all flowing river of blood. There was a hard cut on my spine too that ignited immense pain.

The Co-operative hospital was in full alert when we reached there. The surgeon Dr. George, C.P.Nasimudeen, Pramod Shenoy and Ali were waiting for me despite their Onam holiday. In that stage of semi consciousness I could understand that I was completely smashed to a point of non recoverability. So I tried to impart the information of the miscreants to my nearby comrades. The doctors who gave me first aid could know that a lot of important veins were cut and a micro vascular surgery was immediately needed. They decided to rush me to a specialized hospital at Ernakulum which is 300 kilometers farther. They arranged an ambulance and Dr. Jomon accompanied me to Ernakulum.

The insufferable pain of my spinal chord was the only experience that made me believe that I was still alive. One of my hands and a leg which were hanging where bandaged to its original position by these doctors.

As the party workers on the way got early information about this rush for life they made all arrangements to remove the blocks on the road. Dr. Jayakumar and Dr. Rajappan were ready to take me to the operation theater. There I underwent a surgery. I still remember that I was floating between consciousness and unconsciousness intermittently. Later I could come to know that there were 17 major wounds on my body which the doctors scrupulously cleaned and dressed. It is actually on the second day since the operation, while cleaning the blood stains on my head the nurse could feel a strong alien object struck on my head. It was a nail struck on my skull. It was a shell of a bomb thrown by the goons. The doctors were uncertain whether this nail would tamper my brain. Luckily enough I was saved by a narrow width. But the diaphragm of my left ear was irrecoverably lost.

Now I am alive to write down this horrible memory. I owe my life to the momentum with which my comrades and friends rushed me to hospital. I owe this life to my comrades, leaders, my wife and to the doctors, to the various hospital workers and to my countrymen who didn't rest even for a moment till the surgery was over.

If my almost cut right arm was not operated in time it would have been lost for ever. I now understand the immense help and love from my comrades and the timely help of the others instilled in me a big energy to overcome the attack of the fascists. Even after the recovery I felt a lot of hardship with my tormented body. It is the out and out consolation from the side of the party workers, leaders and the masses that made me overcome the hardship. I still remember with immense gratitude that it is the head load workers of Ernakulam who came forward to give blood to me. I feel proud that I am still living out of that blood. Even after I was discharged from the hospital I had to stay back at Ernakulam for another one month for further treatment. There I was staying in the Deshabhimani building. Amidst continued threats on my life from RSS goons, the comrades in Ernakulam stood in guard till I return to my native place.

Why did I become a target of the RSS goons is quite evident. It is my political activities in my village that provoked them to attempt on my life. The Eastern Kadirur, my village, is now portrayed as a CPM village by the media. Earlier Pattiam Panchayat that includes East Kadirur was a strong hold of old Praja Socialist Party and Congress. They have been ruling this panchayat since 1978. RSS fascists were generously encouraged under their rule. The CPM, other left parties and democrats had to put a persistent defense to save this village from the clutches of fascism. As a result of this struggle Pattiam Panchayat came under the rule of CPM in 1979. RSS people were infuriated at this turn of events and they were left with no other alternative than unleashing violence to regain their lost ground. As a result I became one of their targets

If we go through the incidents that took place in east Kadirur and Pattiam Panchayat one by one within a span of last twenty years we can see how the fascists turned that area their fortress. They started their activities in that area from an 'illam', (traditional house of Brahmin family) the household of the old feudalist, opening a branch of RSS. In sequel to the opening of this branch they unleashed a lot of violent attacks in this region. Party workers Kittichi Rameshan and Sukumaran became martyrs in their attacks. Later they conducted hit and run attacks among the beedi workers of Dinesh Beedi Company who were generally supporting the communists in Pathayakunnu of Pattiam Panchayat. On 6th April 1979 some RSS goons attacked beedi workers of Thalassery taluk. This attack was the implementation of a decision of RSS at the state level. A lot of people assembled from various parts of Kerala took part in this series of attacks conducted on the same day. There were professional killers trained by the RSS. K.V. Balan of Kodiyeri, U.P. Damu of Chambad and Madathil Balan were assassinated in this unexpected attack. Comrade Damu of Eranjippuram was fatally wounded and he was admitted in Medical college hospital, later he succumbed to his wounds. Instead of counter attacks the CPM rallied the people of the panchayat in defense of the RSS violence.

Sreekrishna Jayanti was a festival in Kerala among Hindus till the RSS came to the political scene. The major birthday celebration of the state till then was *Sree Narayana Jayanti* (the birthday of Narayana Guru) widely conducted by Sree Narayana Dharma Paripalana Sangham (SNDP) mainly staging big rallies. After the inception of RSS they started conducting *Sree Krishna Jayanti Procession* in the state. This novel form was adopted to attract children to the Shakhas. Once it so happened that *Sree Krishna Jayanti* and *Onam* festival came together. The RSS people of east Kadirur conducted *Sree Krishna Jayanti* celebration. They arranged a *pookalam* competition (a typical drawing with flowers) for children. *Pookkalam* is a traditional art with flowers drawn mainly by women and children in every house during Onam days. They declared prizes in this competition. They had a hidden agenda to rally the masses in the *Sree Krishna Jayanti procession*. Actually RSS was trying to sneak in to the sentiments of the general public using the *Onam* celebration. The communists of that area could easily smell the danger behind the move of the RSS. They exposed the intention of the RSS through pamphlets. The RSS leadership awaiting the children to come in their camp was unhappy as no children turned up to their celebration. The communists had already conducted a celebration under the banner of *Balasangham* in the UP School of east Kadirur. This celebration was massive and successful. These sorts of continuous resistance from the side of communists infuriarated the RSS leadership further. Decreasing number of participants insisted them to close down the shakha soon. As Communist party had given guidance, people of the panchayat became dare enough to resist any violence from the RSS' side. Once RSS goons dared even to kill Com. M.K.

Surendran, Secretary of the CPM Branch Committee. Yet a consistent and persistent effort of communist helps Pattiyam Panchayat to retain enduring peace. The massive influence of the party in that area is the real reason of the media to portray it as a *Party Village*. The party workers feel proud in it as they have paid immense price for it.

The Master Plan to wipe out the communists and democrats on the one side and enhance the influence of RSS on the other is not confined to a panchayat alone. RSS had a big plan to turn Kannur as their experimental area to crush the communists. Just before the attack on me there was a meeting of RSS at Panoor in which one of their state leaders who was working in Trivandrum expressed his fury as follows: "Since now no more bulbs, the transformers themselves are to be cracked down". This utterance is self evident about the conspiracy of the attack on me. Moreover, the RSS usually adopts a method of defamation campaign. If they want to destroy someone or an institution they usually indulge in propaganda against that individual or institution they targeted. In order to attain this aim they propagate Geebelsian lies in a consistent way so that they can tarnish the image of the targeted among the people. Later I came to know that this tactic was adopted in my case too. A notice was released by the District Committee of the RSS in Kannur. It was alleged that myself and Panoli Valsan were the people behind the assassination of one Mr.Uthaman an RSS. When one of their cadres named Jayakrishnan was killed in broad day light in a class room they alleged that Pinarayi Vijayan, the State Secretary of the party was behind the incident. They portrayed me as the squad leader of the imaginary criminal band who executes that assassination. The notice runs like this: "The conspiratorial role played by CPM State Committee in the assassination of Jayakrishnan is evident. Almost all the evidence collected in this case stands testimony to this. The role played by Jayarajan, the present MLA is to be unearthed. The leader of the criminal band in Kannur, P. Jayarajan is still untouched by the police. The role played by both the leadership of the state committee and of Jayarajan is quite known to the people. P. Jayarajan was present in the District Court of Thalasseri where the accused in this case were awarded capital punishment." This is a sample of their propaganda campaign. They always present those whom they want to annihilate as anti-social and anti-people there by they feel that they can create a priori that will in turn legitimize their brutality.

After my one month stay in Ernakulam for treatment as an out-patient I returned to my native place on November 25th. It was the day to commemorate the martyrs of Koothuparmbu who sacrificed their lives in a firing during the agitation against the wrong educational policy of the Congress lead United Front government. I was there to attend the meeting conducted at Kannur. The chief guests of that meeting were Com. Harkishen Singh Surjeet, the General Secretary of the party and Com. Pinarayi Vijayan, the State Secretary of the party. When I got down at Kannur on 25th November I was a thoroughly changed person in my physical appearance. Everybody came to know that I had a narrow escape from death. As a dear one coming back to life I was given cordial welcome by my comrades.

I continued my treatment this time with physiotherapy at Co-operative Hospital, Thalassery. Dr. C.P. Nazuruddin who gave me first aid at the time of attack was wonder stuck to see me walking towards him. While I was in the hospital in Ernakulam a lot of leaders including Comrade E.K. Nayanar, V.S. Achuthanandan, Pinarayi Vijayan and cadres came to see me and console me in the days of pain and strain. But the visit of Comrade C. Kannan whom I respect the most was of much significance to me. He then told me about the malicious propaganda unleashed by the RSS outside. While I was struggling with death in the hospital bed RSS was portraying me as the organizer of the trade of death. Not only the mainstream media but even the democratic people were misled by this propaganda. They always think CPM is the sole reason for the unrest in Kannur. They often forget that hundreds of CPM cadres and leaders are either killed or mutilated in Kannur. 'The disaster of Kannur' a cover story printed in weekly Mathrubhumi on July 6th, 1998 with big photograph of RSS cadres carrying dandha in their hands is an exclusive example for a misleading propaganda. The caption given to this picture was 'the growing resistance in Kannur'. In that article they described RSS and CPM alike: they portrayed RSS a checkmate to CPM violence. Hence Kannur become a nightmare for the rest of state.

I was the candidate of LDF contesting from Koothuparambu constituency in the Assembly election of 2001. Mr. Ramesh Kumar IAS belonging to Kadappa, Andhrapradesh was the observer of the Election Commission. He was advised by some of his friends not to go to Kannur. Mr. Ramesh Kumar himself had stated that none of these friends were in Kannur before. Unfortunately they got such pictures from the media. Mr. Ramesh Kumar had gone to all the 150 polling stations of the constituency. Later when the election and declaration were over, he told me as follows: "From the information given by my friends I thought that Kannur was a terrible place of bombs. In my experience the election in Kannur was peaceful. Stray incidents that took place even in Kadappa during elections were not seen here. I don't know why the media consider Kannur as a dreadful place."

This shows how the mainstream media distort reality. Mr. Ramesh Kumar IAS is not the only one who gradually changed their opinion on Kannur when became familiar to that place.

While I was in my hospital bed, I had enough time to think about my native district and the significance of the resistance against the fascists. Kannur had a tremendous glorious past of fighting injustice. Its ancient art *theyyam* itself is a manifestation of the relentless struggle for justice. Kannur had played a major role in the fight against foreign imperialism and feudalism. Kannur has produced ever remembering martyrs in these struggles. The people in this district were never apolitical and their political will is indomitable. The recent fight against fascism propounded by RSS is a continuation of old and heroic fight. But the media in Kerala is thinking it otherwise. They are placing both RSS and CPM on the same plank in order to mislead the real political content of the conflicts. I felt a real political exposure of the existing political reality of Kannur is of much importance to the anti fascist struggle going on there. This thought inspired me to the idea of writing this book. Since then I had been collecting materials for this book. The archives of leading Malayalam dailies *Deshabhimani, Mathrubhumi, Malayala Manorama* and *Kerala Kaumudi* helped me in many ways. I got in touch with many significant authors and the various enquiry commission reports on RSS riots. I also got in touch with police administration reports as well as works on RSS that helped me to formulate the ideological approach of this work. I always had a hectic schedule in my day to day political activities. Hence this book was done within the limitation of a full time political activist. This work may have its own limitations and short comings. Yet I earnestly feel this humble work will also have its own place in the general resistance movement against fascism.

I am almost mutilated because of the attack on me. My right arm is numb. My thumb on the left hand is cut off. So I needed a lot of help from others to bring it out in this form. Comrade P.M.Manoj of *Deshabhimani* and Preejith Raj were of immense help to me in writing and editing this book. Sreejith of Kannavam helped me in collecting the materials. I express my gratitude to R. Sreelatha of *Deshabhimani* who did type setting and to all those who helped me in this venture.

P Jayarajan

(This is the foreword written by the author for the Malayalam Edition)

Chapter 1

RSS and the Roots of Fascism

The declared policy of *Rashtreeya Swayam Sevak Sangh* is to turn India to a *Hindu nation*. The method that they adopted to achieve this aim is to wipe out their enemies. This method basically is fascist. RSS claims that it is a socio-cultural organization. In order to analyze this claim, one has to understand the ideology upheld by RSS and the fascist method they undertake to fulfill their aims. A brief understanding of the history of RSS is relevant here.

RSS was formed in 1925 by Dr. Keshav Baliram Hedgewar. Born in Nagpur in 1889 Hedgewar was a student of medical science. But he never practiced what he learned in the Medical College at Calcutta. Hedgewar underwent imprisonment for a small period of time in connection with Non Co-operation Movement. He was a Congress volunteer then. He was in touch with B.S.Moonje and V.D.Savarkar while he was in jail and he had detailed ideological debate with them. Precisely out of this debate he evolved the theory of Hindu Rashtra. After he was released from prison he left his Gandhian politics and started to work for the ideology of Hindu Rashtra. He was against Gandhi's adherence to Muslim cause and his dedication to Hindu-Muslim unity. Hedgewar was not ashamed of being an arch revivalist. In the early days of its inception RSS was an organization following Brahmanic norms. It was always in the offensive and had a military concept along with it. This picture of RSS is clearly depicted in a secret leaflet circulated among Congressmen while it was banned in connection with the murder of Gandhiji. Almost all the leaders of RSS in the early period were Brahmins belonging to Chitpavan sect in Maharashtra.

Astonishingly enough, RSS had looked at the fascists of Italy with all reverence. Mussolini and Hitler were their idols. B.S.Moonje who is considered to be the teacher of Dr. Hedgewar had gone to Italy in 1931. He had a meeting with Mussolini there. His experience of this meeting is scribbled in his diary.

The Hindu revivalists in India were very much fascinated towards Italian fascism and this fascination had its fullest expression in Maharashtra. Articles and editorials extolling Italian fascism and their leader Mussolini had been published in their journal named Kesari. Fascists used to uphold a method of militarization under the leadership of a 'benevolent dictator' which they thought will bring a thorough change in the society. The RSS was much inspired by this fascist methodology. Their ideological affinity to this methodology led B.S.Moonje to visit Italy and meet Mussolini who was totally against the democratic and liberal views of the west. The Italian fascists and their RSS counterparts in India admired fascism as an effective alternative to western democracy.

B.S.Moonje thought that he could make India a Hindu Rashtra by adopting fascist models and methodology. A small book named the *Recent Laws for the Defense of the State* was of much help to him. This book was published in 1928. Even before the publication of this book D.V.Tahmankar who was an ardent follower of Mussolini and the London correspondent of Kesari wrote a biography of Mussolini. A series of articles by Tahmankar on fascism were also published in Kesari in those days.

The fascists all over the world had invariably shared the view that a state run and controlled by a single individual is more effective for social transformation than any modern democracy. The RSS was in total agreement with this fascist theory of Mussolini. That is why RSS adopted a typical organizational form that makes everybody to undergo the dictate of a single leader. *Italy and the Young Generations* was the title of a series of articles published in K*esari* in the year 1929. This series was totally in praise of the fascist organizations in Balilla and Aveng Desthi. These articles minced no word to praise the young Italian generation in their fight and victory against the old one. It was so argued that the victory of this young generation was closely related with their discipline and their reverences to traditional values and staunch religiosity. The concept of women in Italy was very much similar to that of *Manusmriti*. The accepted belief of Italy upheld the theory that women should be protected always and she should not have given the right of divorce and of franchise. The old Indian attitude that the real place of women is the kitchen was also asserted in these articles.

Moonje was generally identified as the brain behind Dr. Hedgewar. Moonje had an irresistible desire to conceive RSS Pan Indian organization. In order to attain the dream he undertook the journey to Italy to learn fascism at its birth place. During his journey in Europe he had visited England, France and Germany. He had been in Italy from March 15 to 24 of 1931. He had a 13 page scribbling of his days in Italy. He had visited the Military College, Fascist Academy of Physical Education and Central Military School of Physical Education. Many time he visited the headquarters of Balilla and Aveng Bestir. His experience in the headquarters was so comprehensive that he spent two full pages to detail it. The aims of these organizations were to instill the spirit of fascism in young blood ranging from age 6-18. They gave military training along with regular physical training. Drills and parades were compulsory for them and they had regular meetings too. The notes in his diary illustrate how much he was fascinated towards the system and functions of these organizations

The Balilla institutions and the conception of the whole organization have appealed to me most, though there is still no discipline and organization of high order. The whole idea is conceived by Mussolini for the military regeneration of Italy: Italians, by nature, appear ease- loving and non-martial like the Indians generally. They have cultivated, like Indians, the work of peace and neglected the cultivation of the art of war. Mussolini saw the essential weakness of his country and conceived the idea of the Balilla organization... Nothing better could have been conceived for the military organization of Italy... The idea of fascism vividly brings out the conception of unity amongst people... India and particularly Hindu India need some such institution for the military regeneration of the Hindus: so that the artificial distinction so much emphasized by the British of martial and non-martial classes amongst the Hindus may disappear. Our institution of Rashtreeya Swayamsewak Sangh of Nagpur under Dr Hedgewar is of this kind, though quite independently conceived. I will spend the rest of my life in developing and extending this Institution of Dr Hedgewar all throughout the Maharashtra and other provinces.

I just saw this morning and afternoon the Balilla and the Fascist Organizations and I was much impressed. Italy needs them for her development and prosperity. I do not see anything objectionable though I have been frequently reading in the newspapers not very friendly criticisms about them and about your Excellency also.

Signor Mussolini: "What is your opinion about them?"

Dr Moonje: "Your Excellency, I am much impressed. Every aspiring and growing nation needs such organizations. India needs them most for her military regeneration. During the British Domination of the last 150 years Indians have been waved away from the military profession. But India now desires to prepare her for undertaking the responsibility for

> her own defense and 1 am working for it. I have already started an organization of my own, conceived independently with similar objectives. I shall have no hesitation to raise my voice from the public platform both in India and England when occasion may arise in praise of your Balilla and Fascist organizations. 1 wish them good luck and every success."

The aggressive Hinduism propagated by RSS is truly evolved from the Italian experiences of Moonje. He is really the master brain to develop the RSS in its Fascist track. Dr. Hedgewar was just obeying the dictates of his Guru, Moonje.

After his return, this great Guru and his disciple worked together to form an all Indian fascist organization. In 1934, a meeting was organized by Mr. Kapte Sasthri. The title of the approach paper was 'Fascism and Mussolini'. It was presided by Dr. Hedgewar and the concluding speech was delivered by Moonje. A series of discussion among Moonje, L. Ghokhale and Hedgewar took place in March 1934. The main theme of the discussion was the militarization of Indian society as already done by fascists both in Italy and Germany.

It is interesting to note that Vinayak Damodar Savarkar, a close associate of Hedgewar and a prominent leader of RSS was much fascinated towards the Nazism of Hitler. His speech in a Hindu Maha Sabha meeting at Madurai was a detailed praise of Nazism. To a great extent Savarkar was in opposition to Nehru as Jawaharlal Nehru was an ardent critic of both Nazism and Fascism.

Regular campaigning named 'Rashtra Jacaranda Atman' was organized by RSS. In those campaigns they used to distribute pamphlets explaining the aims of RSS. They introduced themselves as a voluntary organization established by renowned revolutionary Dr. Kesava Belram Hedgewar. All the leaders explained the propagation of Hindu thought by RSS as a 'Yuga Dharma' (Mission of the Epoch). These leaders believed that the RSS is really the voluntary spirit of *Swayam Sevak*. They propagated that if Hindu is awakened the world too is awakened and they felt that 'Sangh

Pariwar' is born for it. They present themselves as if they stand for religious freedom and equality for all sections.

Even though they say such rosy words about themselves the real essence of their ideology is evolved not only from Nazism and Fascism but also from many other despotic and revivalist ideologies. Now an organization by name 'Sanatana Dharma Swayam Sevak Sangh' is working in Burma in order to instill new spirit to RSS in India. This organization had a link with the military committee of Burma. And this military committee is one of the dreaded drugs mafia of the world. They can raise funds for the function of RSS in India.

The origin and growth of RSS took place during the time of struggle for Independence. Hence it is interesting to learn the role played by the RSS towards the Struggle for Independence. Astonishingly enough, RSS had a lethargic attitude towards the Independence struggle. Instead, they had a curious position towards the minorities in India. In the official documents of the freedom struggle RSS was the least mentioned force. They were not anti imperialists and their pro imperialist posture is quite evident in history.

Both the founder leaders of RSS, Dr. Hedgewar and Golwalker, were least interested in the struggle for independence. In 1947 when the British were about to leave India Golwalker supported the British in his speech in the Anniversary meeting of RSS. He said that the opposition of British governance comes out of parochialism. He even went to the extent of supporting the British in order to oppose Gandhi.

Yet it is seen that Hedgewar once participated in a satyagraha led by Gandhiji. This participation was absolutely his own decision that didn't have any relationship with the RSS. After the formation of RSS Hedgewar wrote and thought only about a Hindu organization. He hadn't any perspective of a modern state. Even RSS itself accepts it as we can see from a journal named *Sangh Pariksha Ke Beej.*

An anthology of Golwalkar named *Sree Guruji Samahar Darshan* was published in 1960. It is evident from this anthology that Golwalkar was least bothered about the struggle for independence. He says in it:

> A lot of people were really inspired by the slogan of sending the British out. But now there are no more British in India and the old spirit is no more here. Now we can question whether the earlier enthusiasm against the British was scientific. We take our oath on religion and culture and there is no mention of British in it.

RSS never accepted independence, secularism, federalism as the basic elements of democracy. As an organization RSS always opposes the modern democratic values. The slogan 'one leader, one flag, and one ideology' propounded by RSS was actually derived from fascism of Italy and Nazism of Germany. This slogan is counter posed against modern democracy. RSS can never accept secularism as a theory. In his autobiography 'Bunch of Thought' Mr. Golwalker categorically expressed his position on these subjects. There is a chapter which completely depict the internal challenges that India faces. Both Muslims and Christians of this nation are illustrated as enemies of India. He also explains how the communists are enemies of this nation.

Our constitution upholds federalism. But RSS is theoretically against the concept of federalism. In the same way RSS is against the tri-color national flag too. In *The Organizer*, the mouth piece of RSS, Golwalker had categorically stated that the national flag of India should be saffron. He was of opinion that India should be renamed as Hindustan which is the synonym of Hindu Rashtra. A day before Indian Independence Golwalker wrote an article In *The Organizer* rejecting the idea of a federal nation. As far as he is concerned only the Hindus can claim to be the real citizens and a real nation should be found on the culture and ideology of Hindus. The political position of modern India is that of upholding the franchise right as a fundamental right. This position of our constitution too is not acceptable to RSS. Thus right from its inception, RSS was against the federal nature of our nation. Even now they are not changed.

RSS even goes to the extent of curtailing the human and civil rights of the minority. In his book *We or Our Nationhood Defined* Golwalker shamelessly embraces the Nazi cultural and national ideology propagated by Hitler. Golwalkar is of opinion that one has to learn a fine lesson from the genocide on Jews by Hitler.

RSS does not have a formal written constitution or an elected and collective leadership. They do not have even an infrastructure prone to democratic elections. In the beginning they didn't have a membership register. Even after 25 years of inception RSS didn't have a written constitution of its own. Hence the membership of anyone in RSS can not be proved. The only available evidence of the membership of RSS is the handbook used by its organizers. Only a few branches of RSS kept membership registers. Except these few registers only the photographs of the route marches conducted by RSS is the evidence of its membership. Nathuram Vinayak Godsey, the assassin of Gandhiji was said to be not a member of RSS, though he had link with RSS at that time. As there is no membership register kept by the Sangh they could easily put forth such an argument. RSS is not even registered as a charitable trust. It doesn't have a bank account and hence not paying any income tax. In short, RSS follows an organizational pattern very much similar to an anarchic organization. The supreme leader of the Sangh is called *Sir Sangh Chalak*. He is the last word and final authority of RSS. There is a working committee under him. The fund collection of RSS is obtained from individuals and *gurudakshina*.

There is an Akhil Bharateeya Representative Sabha existing under the leadership of the Central Committee of the RSS. The supreme leader convenes the meeting of the committee every month at Nagpur. Any Swayam Sevak above 18 years is eligible to attend this meeting. Generally the leaders are either from Brahmins or upper caste Hindus. Just below this Sabha there is a zonal committee then a state committee, divisional committee, city committee and at the bottom the branch committee. Appointed organizers are in-charge of day to day affairs of the committee at city level. They are known as Pracharaks and they play a prominent role in the activities of the Sangh. These organizers are deputed in various places according to the need. The general workers have to take dictates from these organizers and they in turn obey the command of the supreme commander, the Sir Sangh Chalak. There cannot be much organizational freedom in this pattern. This form of function is well defined by Golwalkar as follows:

> The need of any election is unwanted if we realize that we are part of the organization and follow its discipline. If asked to play Kabadi then do it. If asked to conduct meeting then do it. Some of our persons were asked to work in politics. It does not mean that they have interest and motivation in it. They will not die as a fish outside water. They won't have any hesitation if they are asked to return. Their rationality is not needed in these matters.

These quoted words of the supreme leader are clear evidences how far the organizational power is centralized in RSS. Here the organizers are mere tools in the hands of the leader. They are bound to execute whatever he wants. The only thing that these organizers are expected to safeguard is that the organizations under their control should not go out of the plank of the *Hindu Rashtra* concept envisaged by the supreme leader. The organizers need only to stick on the fascist principles given by the supreme leader. It be comes very clear from the words of Golwalker uttered in a meeting on 5th March 1960 at Indore.

> Some of our workers are working in the political scenario. There they have to arrange meetings, conduct processions and render slogans according to its need. These activities might not have anything to do with our organizational works.

> However, they should use their maximum ability there as an actor in a drama. But RSS won't tolerate if somebody goes beyond the limit stipulated by the leader.

RSS at any cost can't go beyond the dictates of a single leader known as Sir Sangh Chalak. Hence a democratic function is virtually impossible in it. This supreme leader has got his own concept of implanting RSS people in various cover organizations too. The former form of BJP was Jan Sangh. It was formed in 1951. From the very beginning RSS was leading the Jan Sangh. RSS commands each and every activity of the Sangh Pariwar through their cunningly implanted organizers. Quite often, there came a lot of conflicts among the views upheld by these organizers and the general masses of Sangh Pariwar. Even elder RSS leaders like Balraj Madhok have mentioned these conflicts in detail.

Actually this is the fascist methodology adopted by RSS to lead its various cover organizations including BJP. Despite the internal conflicts, the reins of these organizations are always controlled by the supreme leader of RSS. This sort of function invariably leads to the formation of various groups within the organization. BJP had ruled this nation for 6 years. While in power many of its leaders became corrupted. More over, a large section of them are affected by the anarchic tendencies too. Kerala is no exception for this rule. In Kerala too BJP is a divided camp of various groups and the predominant group in it is RSS. Here we have experience that these different groups are alleging corruption against each other. Now the old workers of RSS have revealed that the conflict within BJP of Kerala was on the corrupt practices of the leaders.

As mentioned earlier RSS has a conspicuous view of fighting the communists. For the same, Golwalker had formulated a theory. According to that theory RSS won't generally fight the communists in public. Instead of doing that, they will give shape to a lot of cover organizations and they will in turn try to cripple the wings of communism. In Kerala there are a dozen of such organizations functioning where hundreds of RSS organizers are implanted. In Kerala RSS has got huge piles of arms. They have got the ability to organize immense funds from outside. They use Maharashtra, Karnataka and Tamilnadu as a rear force supporting the activities of RSS in Kerala. They have even wide infrastructure to treat wounded men in hospitals and to arrange hideout for their cadres. Comparatively speaking, the strength of RSS both in Maharashtra and Kerala is almost the same. In Kerala RSS have 1381 mandalam committees. A mandalam is virtually equal to a Panchayat. They have got 1113 Shakhas altogether under which 4273 sub Shakhas are also functioning. The foremost cover organization of RSS was Rashtreeya Sevika Samiti established in 1936. But its students' wing by name Akhil Bharateeya Vidhyarthi Parishad was organized in 1948 was the ideal one. In addition to that they have got the Bharateeya Masdur Sangh organized for workers. This workers organization was established in 1955. And in 1978 they formed a Kissan organization. Later, exclusively to organize adivasis they founded two organization named Vanavasi Vikas Kendra and Adivasi Sangh. They have one NGO Centre, National Teachers Union and National Federation of College Teachers. Further, in order to consolidate the religious sentiments of the people they gave birth to Vishwa Hindu Parishad, Temple Protection Vedi, Vishaal Hindu Sammelan, Virad Hindu Samaj, Hindu Samajolsav, Hindu Front, Hindu Manch, Hindu Jagaran Vedika, United Hindu Vedi etc. They have an exclusive organization aiming children named Balagokulam. On social welfare area they have their celebrated Seva Bharati, Vanavasi Kalyan Ashram, Vidhyaniketan, Vivekananda Kendra, Deen Dayal Research Institute etc. On intellectual front they have Bharateeya Vichara Kendra and Tapasya which give special concern to cultural and literary activities. In the area of elder women they have their Matrumandalam. On religious education they have established Amrita Bharati and on medical front they have the Vivekananda Medical Mission functioning. In addition to these institutions, they have established a bunch of journals under their control. In Kerala they have Janmabhoomi, a daily and Kesari, a weekly. Vritandam and Pragaty are their monthlies. Kurukshetram and Jaybharatam are their publication wings in Kerala. The Jan Sangh which was merged in Janata Party in the post emergency period was never revived. Instead BJP was formed later. Today BJP is the vast front organization of the RSS. RSS has got a thorough ideological and political infrastructure to control all these organizations floated around.

RSS is silent on their economic sources to keep all these mass organizations functioning. Everybody knows that RSS cannot fund these organizations out of the regular collection and menial Gurudakshinas. Investigations have categorically proved that they are getting immense economic assistance from foreign countries.

As mentioned earlier, the Sangh Pariwar has an anarchic organizational set up. Hence a lot of undesirable tendencies are cropping up in the form of corruption in these organizations. RSS had to sacrifice hundreds of its organizers on this account. The RSS do not receive foreign funds as such. Instead they have given shape to charitable organizations which are usually dealing with these matters.

RSS has a sister organization named Friends of India Society in America. This society as well as Hindu Swayam Sevak Sangh is formed in tune of the Hindu agenda of RSS. In such a way the Viswa Hindu Parishad in India have an equivalent in America, the Viswa Hindu Parishad of America. Similarly BJP too is having a counterpart in America by name Overseas Friends of BJP. IDRF is an organization that gives assistance to various other organizations in India. Their Seva International is the main organization arranging international monetary assistance to RSS. Assimilation of such an enormous international fund by RSS is generally quite unknown to the public. These activities are quite concealed in nature. There are no documents being kept for the amazing funds. The distribution of this concealed wealth is done by the Sir Sangh Chalak. RSS is assisting fishermen and Tribal people from the consolidated fund.

"Hindus in India are always attacked and intimidated" is a usual cry by the RSS. This is a planned propaganda to project their activities as actions in self–defence. RSS claims that tolerance and peace are the trademarks of Hinduism. But in the name of the self defence RSS practices aggressive activities. A series of armed attacks is being carried out by RSS towards the minorities in India. They consider these aggressive activities as pious deed done to safeguard the interest of Hindus. Guruji Golwalkar who was the supreme leader of RSS had justified the genocide of Jews by Hitler as a great patriotic activity. Picking up the thread from both Nazism and Fascism B.S..Moonje had once said "We are preparing our boys in the game of massacre with the sole aim of victory". In short this game is being taught in the drills of RSS.

The functioning of RSS too is interesting. Whenever they feel their influence among the people is getting down they rely on the politics of violence. To them violence is a means to regain the lost influence. Government of India has a lot of enquiry commission reports on communal riots, where the part played by RSS is quite evident. The Jagmohan Committee Report on the Ahmadabad riot in 1969, Madan Commission Report on Bheewandi riot in 1970, Justice Vithayathil Commission Report on Thalasseri riot in 1971, Jithendra Narain Commission Report on Jamshedpur riot in 1979 and Justice P. Venugopal Commission Report on Kanyakumari riot in 1982 are a few among them. In all these reports, the role played by RSS is comprehensively narrated. It is interesting to note that RSS is practicing a strange methodology for social dominance. In the beginning they draw a line of demarcation between various religious communities living in a place. Then they start attacking the minority in these places. There by they can draw a clear line between majority Hindus and minority community. They know very well that the minority section will realign them when their very existence is threatened. According to it the majority community is also is consolidated. When such a clear line of demarcation is drawn, it becomes easy for RSS to come to the forefront in the name of the protectors of Hinduism.

This is a clear cut agenda of the RSS from very inception in 1925.

RSS is being led by the ideology of violence. In every communal riot there is polarization that can be consolidated in terms of religion. History shows that Viswa Hindu Parishad and Bajrang Dal, the two wings of Sangh Pariwar were born out of communal riots. These two organizations helped BJP to come to power in Delhi. The Sangh Pariwar will start their designed attacks on the minority communities and their institutions and will make a convenient plank for BJP to come to power. Actually the institutions of BJP are built on the tombs of the massacre of the minority. Strangely enough, this Sangh Pariwar forces continue their aggressive policies towards minorities even after BJP is put to power. 116 attacks against Christian minority were reported during Jan.98 to Feb.99. All these attacks were carried out mainly against the schools and churches of the minority. Even Christian priests and nuns were not spared in these attacks. South Asian Human Right Commission reports on these attacks as follows:

> "Almost all the attacks are organized and lead by individuals having close association with Sangh Pariwar. Sangh Pariwar's associates were ruling in those places during these attacks. BJP, VHP, Bajarangh Dal, Hindu Jagaran Manch are the members of Sangh Pariwar".

Hence the history of RSS in the post independence era is surely the history of aggression and violence against minorities in India.

Chapter 2

The Devilish Path Trodden by Fascists in Kerala

Originated in Maharashtra, RSS became very popular in Maratha - Hindi belt in India. But it took a long time to reach Kerala. The strong presence of various reformation movements as well as Communist Party in Kerala were stumbling block in the growth of RSS in Kerala. Hence it was a late comer, the communist in Kerala, who were always very vigilant about the threat posed by the RSS.

Kerala had a long history of renaissance movement. Swami Vivekananda had a brief visit to Kerala during the end of 19th century. The social life then prevailed in this state gave him a horrible picture of communal division that prompted him to call Kerala 'a lunatic asylum.' He could easily identify the state of Kerala as the most backward in Indian states. Swamiji felt very awkward towards the caste feelings prevailed in Kerala as well as untouchability and the superstitions existed then. The untouchability among the Hindu sections on those days in Kerala was so intense and brutal that the majority of the people were cruelly oppressed.

The 19th century witnessed the missionary activities of the Christian communities in Kerala. In the year 1805 London Mission Society started its work in Kerala, Further Church Mission Society started its work in the northern part of Travancore. The Salvation Army started their work in the southern part of Travancore. Basel Evangelical Mission of Germany was the predominant missionary agency in the Malabar area. Though all these missions were aiming at the propagation of their religion, luckily enough they introduced education as a tool of propaganda.

The activities of these missionaries were welcomed by the downtrodden section of the society as it gave them a solace in a society where untouchability was predominant. The working community of Kerala were even prepared to accept Christianity as it took them out of the caste ridden system of untouchability. In short, the missionary activities of these agencies emancipated the downtrodden sections of the people to a new realm of independence. At the same time the radicals among the upper castes dared enough to criticize the undesirable practices of untouchability. But the conservative sections among the upper caste could not sit idle towards this great transformation. The newly born idea of freedom amidst the poor people was unbearable to them. As a result of this, there were a lot of riots in 1829 throughout southern parts of Travancore. There were a lot of attacks against newly converted Christians. Their church and educational institutions were left to nadir. On one such occasion even army was called for to put down such a riot in Kollam in the year 1859. The police force and the government machinery were siding with the conservative sections of the caste Hindus at the time of riots.

The emancipation attained by the backward communities in Kerala in those time was so intense that it could bring long lasting social awareness among the people. Temples were the citadels of knowledge and culture at that time. But these temples were unapproachable to the backward communities because of the conservative ideology of untouchability. As a result, the social wealth of culture and knowledge were unavailable to the vast majority of the people. In short, there were no temples or places of worship for the outcasts. It is at this moment in the year 1888 Sree Narayana Guru, a Hindu monk and a social reformer in Kerala established a temple of Lord Shiva on the shore of River Neyyar in the southern part of Travancore. In those times, the lower caste people were not allowed to establish temples and to conduct rituals there. Brahmins were considered to be the sole authority to do so. It is in defiance of this conservative idea Narayana Guru installed a Shiva Temple. This act of the Guru aroused great opposition and contempt from the cast Hindus. At the same time, another Hindu monk Chattambi Swami who was a contemporary of Narayana Guru, started his activities against cast Hindu ideologies among upper castes. These two efforts aligned together to make a big impact on the entire process of reformation. Soon the caste system and the untouchability were considered to be inhuman and hence against progress. Meantime there arose a movement under the leadership of Dr. Palpu for the admission of lower caste students to educational institutions and government services. All these efforts culminated in the formation of SNDP in the year 1903. SNDP was a movement established by Narayana Guru for the emancipation of mainly the Ezhava section, a backward cast.

The great October Revolution had its impact all over the world in the struggle against monarchy and dynasty. The emergence of a socialist regime under the leadership of Communist Party in Russia instilled a lot of hope among the poor all over the world. In Kerala also, the great October Revolution had its impacts. In those days there was stiff fight between reformers and conservatives in Kerala social life. Very often these struggles took the form of confrontation on streets. These confrontations were generally known as Nair-Ezhava riots. T.K.Madhavan the Asst. Secretary of SNDP then was a national leader too. In the meeting of the Congress at Kakinada, Madhavan issued pamphlets requesting the Congress to take a staunch position in the matter of untouchability. T.K. Madhavan himself being a member of the

Ezhava community of Kerala was a victim of the social evils. After the Kakinada meeting, he had a detailed discussion with Mahatma Gandhi. It is after that discussion Gandhiji decided to launch a movement against untouchability also. Now we can say that it is the Kerala experience that opened the eyes of national leadership of Congress on the issue of untouchability. Some of the leaders of this reformation movement of Kerala like Sahodaran Ayyappan had a lenience towards the new socialist state of Russia and they preached in detail about the emergence of proletarian class and of Lenin to their followers. While these movements were taking shape in Travancore a reformation movement, in parallel to this, was taking shape in northern Kerala under the leadership of Brhamananda Sivayogi. This movement of Sivayogi was more rational than that in Travancore. Sooner Sivayogi got a lot of disciples and Vagbhatananda was the foremost among them.

Nair community of the erstwhile Travancore belonged to the upper strata of the society. They could attain literacy earlier. As a result of this, there emerged a series of reformation movements. Nair Service Society was formed in the year 1915, under the leadership of Mannathu Padmanabhan. Sri. K. Kelappan who was a leader of reformation movements of Malabar was the first president of the Nair Service Society and this society under the leadership of both Padbhanabhan and Kelappan unleashed a lot of struggle against the then prevailing customs in the Nair caste such as the matrilineal property right.

Along with the emergence of this great renaissance a new movement was taking place among the *Pulaya* community considered to be the most bottom level community of Kerala. In the year 1907 an organization , Sadhujana Paripalana Yogam (organization for the poor) was established by Ayyankali. Meantime there was such a movement taking place in Cochin also under the leadership of K.P. Karuppan. These different movements converged in the year 1913 in the formation of Pulaya Maha Sabha. The Araya community was a group of fishermen throughout the sea shore of southern Kerala and was an oppressed section in society. In the year 1908 they also had their own organization on the basis of their caste division aiming at economic and educational emancipation. And sooner, there was the Akila Kerala Araya Mahajana Sabha established in the year 1922 under the leadership of Dr. Velukutty Arayan. While all the castes were aiming at a new horizon of development, the Muslim community of Kerala was also thriving for its own progress. Vakkom Abdhulkhadar Maulavi took the lead of a reformation movement among Muslims in Kerala in those days.

The beginning of 20th century was an epoch making stage in the history of Kerala. The social life of Kerala was divided on caste lines and the urge for social change started among the oppressed castes. The ruling class of Kerala then was undoubtedly the Namboodiri caste. They were the rulers and owners of land as well as of culture. The struggle against caste system in Kerala and the new development among oppressed castes generally aimed at the domination of Namboodiri caste in Kerala. Hence it was natural that this Brahmin community was totally against the reformation process going on in the society. But 20th century was a century of change and the storm of this change uprooted the old concepts of casteism among various castes of Kerala and strangely enough, Namboodiri caste was also no exception. The Yogakshema Sabha which was established in 1909 spearheaded the renaissance movements among the Namboodiri community of Kerala. And thus the entire social system of Kerala was undergoing a great change during the period of the first decades of the great 20th century.

Precisely on the ground of these immense social reformations among almost all the castes in Kerala, resulted in the emergence of a new social environment in Kerala. In thisenvironment there emerged in Thiruvananthapuram the Communist League during 1930-31 the seeds of early communism was sown. The Communist League that championed the formation of Communist Party was established during 1930-31. This league didnot have any direct access or organizational link with the Communist Party on the national level. But it was a consolidated expression of the countless progressive thoughts that was proliferating among all strata of society. In the year 1934 Congress Socialist Party was formed in Kerala uniting various persons having leanings towards socialism and was still working along with the Congress. It is just after the formation of Congress Socialist Party, the communists of Kerala began communication with the communists at the national level. A small nucleus of a communist party was formed in Kerala within the Congress Socialist Party. In those days there was a continuous rapport between the leadership of both Congress Socialist Party as well as Communist Party in the national level and both these parties had common views on various issues that enabled them to work together at national level. In Kerala, the Communists were part in the social reformation that was going in various community organizations like NSS and SNDP. At the same time the Communists organized the workers against the ruthless oppression of the then prevailing social hierarchy. By undertaking this dual task of social reformation and class struggle among workers, Communists could establish a lot of peasants and workers organizations throughout Kerala and thus the Communist movement indirectly contributed to the renaissance movement championed by the community organizations and in the emancipation of the people enslaved in the caste system of Kerala. Though started belatedly, when comparing with other parts of India, the renaissance movement of Kerala could grow in a faster pace that it could reject the conservative ideas of castiesm from the general polity of Kerala society. The Communists were an immediate sequel to this renaissance movement and thus could easily consolidate the values of renaissance to the general milieu of class struggle.

The renaissance movements of Kerala originated by social organizations such as NSS, SNDP, Yogakshema Sabha etc. were further carried on by the Communists of Kerala. The castiesm kept human being as bonded laborer and renaissance was a process that transformed the bonded labor to a new human being. The socialist ideology attributed by the communists to the total ideological realm of reformation once again transformed this new human being to a further new socialistic human being. In the first part of this book I made some attempts to elaborate the ideological kernel of RSS and their leaning towards neo fascism and Nazism. Both these ideologies from Italy and Germany were strongly based on national pride of an old fashion. But Kerala polity had improved much out of its renaissance movement so that the ideological premises of RSS was very much backward when compared with the Malayalee sensibility. So it was almost impossible for the RSS to find out a place of their own in the ideological realm of Malayalees. The RSS were always considered to be either secondary or 'not up to mark' people in Kerala. So it took a lot of time for the RSS to extend its venomous roots in Kerala.

In the 1940 while RSS was trying to reach Kerala, they could understand the hurdles awaiting them in advance. They could also understand that the modus operandi adopted in other states could not help them here. So instead of expressing their existence in this state through some incidents, they tried to organize people in Kerala in a secret and planned way. They started work in Kerala in the year 1942, that too from Malabar. Malabar was supposed to be less influenced by the renaissance movements of Kerala because of its connection with Madras government. RSS thought it easier to find its space in Malabar but their expectation was shattered soon despite the presence of fifty eight percentage of Hindus there.

In 1940 M.S.Golwalker was the Sir Sangh Chalak of RSS. He sent two RSS volunteers to Kerala in order to start their function in the State in 1942. D. V. Tengdi, one among them was deputed to Malabar. The other one was Madhukar Oku to whom the charge of Travancore was given. However the activity of Tengidi in

Malabar could find some results. He could start the first RSS 'Shakha' in Calicut with the help of one P.K.M. Raja. The first Shakha was functioning in Raja's domestic compound which was later shifted to Ganapati High School ground of Chalappuram. The Mukhya Shikshak of that Shakha in which there were 12 members, P.Kumaran was one among them. Three RSS Cadres from Kerala took part in the training camp conducted by RSS at Nagpur in 1942. After the training camp with the help of these Malayalees, RSS succeeded in establishing their second Shakha at Calicut. The entire expense towards this training of Malayalees and establishing the Shakhas was met with the Nagpur head quarters. Later some other Shakhas were also formed in Calicut.

There was an all India meeting of RSS at Madurai in 1942. In that winter session workers from Kerala region were included. As stated before, RSS had a very clandestine style of function in Kerala. First of all, they endeavour to identify some as close associate. Then they start their whispering campaign. It was to avoid confrontation in the beginning. RSS was quite sure that they were lagging behind the general secular and democratic fabric of Kerala. They tried to find their influential areas among the fishermen community of Meenchantha, Thiruvallur and Vellai of Calicut. The Araya community of that place were Hindu fishermen. RSS gave ample money to them to purchase country boats and fishing nets and tried to woo that community to their hold as the Arayas of that locality was less influenced by the social transformation of the state. In that way in its beginning, RSS made use of the backwardness as well as their poverty. During this stage Golwalker sent his third man Mr.Vasanth Gokhale to Kerala. He was sent to Palakkadu as Pracharak and the fourth one Mr. Anand Vidwan deputed to Cochin as the first Vistarak. Meanwhile Mr.Tengidi was concentrating his entire efforts in Thalasseri. Thalasseri had a typical blend of secularism. Almost all the traders of the town belonged to Muslim community and most of them with a secular mindset. Mr. Tengidi while concentrating his work in Thalasseri unleashed a secret campaign to portray these traders as anti Hindu and anti nation. RSS advised their limited followers to curb the growth of Muslim community of traders in Thalasseri. Since then they had a concerted organizational attempt in Thalasseri that tried to draw a communal division between Muslims and non Muslims of that area. In the year 1943 just after one year of their first Shakha in Calicut, RSS conducted an industrial training camp, the first of its kind, at Calicut. Though it was a small one M.S.Golwalker himself participated in it. His participation showed their interest to have a foothold in Kerala region. In 1944 one more Vistharak Sadasiv Danke was sent to Trichur. In 1944 there was an officers camp at Nagpur where P.Kumaran was appeared as the first Mukhya Shikshak from Kerala. Mean time, Tengidi was shifted to Bengal and Mr. Shankar Shastri was posted in his place. In continuation of this B.Rao, M.Dev and D.Dedol were appointed as organizers in Cochin, Trivandrum and Trichur respectively. RSS could find out 5 Malayalee Pracharaks In 1946. They were P.Kumaran, T.N.Bharatan, P.Madhavan, R.Venugopal and Marthanda Varma.

As mentioned earlier, Communism was the predominant ideology in Kerala. RSS is an ideological instrument of Hinduism as envisaged by Hedgewar. Having an ideology of its own RSS always tried to be ideologically predominant. Hence RSS launched a fight on the basis of its ideology against any other ideology that is coming on their way. As the Communist ideology is predominant in Kerala, it is quite natural that RSS will fix the communists as their number one enemy. So a fight against communism in Kerala was a deliberate approach adopted by RSS. A direct fight against communists in Kerala is not feasible because of the weakness of RSS. So they tried to have a rapport with other social organizations in Kerala. In the beginning RSS thought that they could easily bring the Hindu community of Travancore under their hold. But soon they realized that the NSS and SNDP are hindrances in their way. Later, RSS leadership could cunningly woo the leaders of both these organizations. In 1950, Mr. Mashij was sent to Alappuzha. Mr. Kamalji Gupta was deputed to Kottayam. Both these organizers were from Jammu. Mr. Gopalan who was a trader and a close associate of the late R. Shankar was the man who helped RSS to start a Shakha in Kollam. -Gopalan was also accepted by RSS as an organizer for a short time span. Like SNDP, NSS also helped RSS to start their Shakha. Both these organizations gave their school buildings to conduct RSS programmes. A district level leader of SNDP was of immense help to RSS in their work in Alappuzha. In Kottayam Mr. Venugopal was working as the Pracharak. Kottayam is an area where Christian population is the majority. In order to win over the Hindus there, the RSS propagated anti-Christian sentiments. Mr. P. Parameswaran of Bharateeya Vichara Kendra was sent to Trivandrum as a Pracharak in 1950. In the years from 1940-50, RSS adopted various efforts and strategies to get themselves into Kerala politics. In 1950, they gave birth to Hindu Maha Mandal and the first meeting of it was conducted at Kollam. Both NSS and SNDP supported RSS in this venture. The formation of this Hindu Maha Mandal was a secret effort of RSS to appease both NSS and SNDP and to portray themselves as a cultural organization.

Apart from the organizational work, RSS had a notion of an ideological apparatus too. They published the weekly, Kesari on November 27th of 1951. Kesari was the sole instrument then to express the ideological convictions of RSS to the people. It is interesting to note here that RSS was against the formation of a united Kerala, right from 1950. Kesari was a flagship in their fight against united Kerala. RSS could envisage in the beginning itself that a unified Kerala will harm their interests. They thought a divided Kerala will be more convenient for implementing their divisive agenda. They were propagating different views in different parts of Kerala according the communal division of the locality.

So it is natural that they were against the unification process of all Malayalees.

The connivance of RSS with SNDP was more evident from the first ever all Kerala camp conducted by RSS in the year 1950 at Sree Narayana College ground in Kollam. There is still another tangible proof to prove this unholy alliance. RSS had an anti cow-slaughter signature campaign in the year 1952. Then R. Shankar, leader of SNDP, sent a circular in support of this campaign to its members. NSS and SNDP were thinking that the Hindu Maha Mandal and the Democratic Congress formed in those days would politically help them to come to power. RSS also had great ambition on these organizations then. But the concerted efforts of all these three groups could not produce any result because of the rejection of these conservative ideas both by the followers of NSS and SNDP. As the effort of RSS done during 1940s were tragically defeated by the people of Kerala, they rejuvenated the Bharateeya Jan Sangh in 1953. Since then Jan Sangh was the political instrument of RSS in Kerala till the formation of BJP.

Though the RSS started its function in Kerala during 1940s, it could not have an indigenous Kerala committee till 1964. The unified Kerala came into being in 1956. But RSS could form an adhoc state committee only in 1958. Mr. Bhaskar Rao was the leader of it. In 1964 there came into being an indigenous state committee to RSS with N. Govinda Menon as State Sangh Chalak and Adv. T.P. Anandan as Karyavahak.

The year 1957 was a landmark in Kerala politics. The first general election after the united Kerala was conducted in that year. The Communist Party had come to power in Kerala. Almost all the anti communist forces of Kerala were wonder struck by this development. Moreover, the communist government started their pro-people activities such as land reforms and introducing social justice in the field of education. Both these steps adopted by the communists infuriated the conservative section of the society. All the land lords and all the clergymen as well as SNDP and NSS united against communist and they wanted the government to be dismissed. With this aim in their mind they started a long agitation by name Vimochana Samaram (liberation struggle). The RSS was very happy with this turn of events as they are basically anti communists. With least hesitation they joined the bandwagon of anti-communism and staged a series of violent incidents of their own. There was a meeting in support of these struggle conducted at Kottayam where Atal Bihari Vajpayee was one among the orators. That meeting was chaired by Mamman Mappila of Malayala Manorama. As a result of this agitation, the newly formed government was dismissed on 31st July 1959 by the Central Government. RSS celebrated this victory on August 1 as 'Vijayadinam' (Victory Day)

Since 1960, RSS was more prone to its Hindutwa agenda in Kerala. They made a communal division in Kerala and argued that the Muslim religion could acquire more power than Hindus. By unleashing Vishwa Hindu Parishad and Temple Protection Samiti in 1966 and forming ABVP in 1964 establishing BMS in 1967, RSS continued its anti-Muslim propaganda throughout Kerala.

Once various forces where assimilated RSS started its violence against communism in Kerala. In order to attack the communists they propagated that the communism and the party were alien to Hindu culture and Hindu nationalism. From the Italian and German experiences RSS knew how to put down communists through neo fascism. With this agenda of opposing communism in their mind RSS people started unleashing violent attacks on communists in Kerala. The documents available in the legislature show that during the period January 1978-March 1979 164 clashes took place in Kerala where RSS was on one side. It is during this period CPI(M) demanded a discussion on the floor of the assembly on this issue. Accordingly on 3rd April 1979 a meeting of the Business Advisory Committee of the Legislature was held. Then Mr. T.N.Bharatan as the organizer of RSS wrote a letter to the then Chief Minister asking him not to conduct a discussion on the floor as there was no representation of RSS or BJP there. While representing things with the higher ups, RSS never retreated from its violent attacks on the communists.

It was after a long time the CPM came to power in Kerala in 1980. RSS found it a convenient time to be more aggressive to create an atmosphere of chaos in this state. With this feeling in their heart they ignited violence throughout the state and as a result of which, there were a lot of clashes both in Thiruvananthapuram and Kollam. In order to tarnish the image of the left government, for the first time in the history of Kerala, RSS came direct under their own banner with a struggle. On 25th March 1980 they conducted a *Dharna* in front of the Govt. Secretariat against the government.

BJP was formed in the year 1980 and its state unit was inaugurated on 15th April. The national leadership of BJP sent a three men delegation consisting of Ram Jath Malani, Bhai Mahaveer M.P. and Jana Krishna Moorthy to enquire the 'Marxist violence' in the state in the same year. During this time the RSS continued their attacks. The CPI(M) was holding the home portfolio of the government. These sorts of continuous attacks as well as the sham enquiry commission, tarnished the image of the home department to a certain extent.

During the year 1981 RSS conducted 771 attacks in Kerala in of which 23 CPM activists were killed and 401 were fatally injured. In addition to these attacks there were a series of theft in temples too. All these added together created an unpleasant atmosphere in the field of law and order. The RSS goons were supposed to behind the concerted temple theft in those days.

A group of Congress MLAs who were supporting the Government of 1980 withdrew the support for their own reasons. A Government of UDF came to power in the year 1981. This shift of the Government gave ample chance to the RSS to grow in the state. This was culminated in the organization of Vishwa Hindu Sammelan at Cochin in1982. In this meeting the RSS adopted some basic changes in their approach towards Kerala politics. This time they gave special attention to temples and their assets. They adopted a propaganda that the Government of the state is giving undue consideration to other religions and neglecting the interest of Hindus in the state. The RSS was actually targetting the Parliament election of 1984 and exclusively for that purpose they gave shape to Hindu Munnani (Hindu Front). This newly found organization contested the elections to State Assembly in 1987 too. Though they could make some headway with this Hindu Munnani they failed to win a single seat either in Assembly or Parliament. The RSS disillusioned once again. In April 1987 RSS started a daily, Janmabhoomi and a monthly, Pragati. Besides these publications there were two other publishing companies Jayabharatam and Kurukshetra sponsored by RSS during this period. All these publications invariably tried to instill Communal and anti Communist sentiments among people. The organizational part of the RSS was controlled by the Sanghchalak and the propaganda wing by the Pracharak. The propaganda wing is assigned with the responsibility of day to day activity as well as conducting violent attacks. The other section is to coordinate the various frontal organizations. From its own experience up to 1980 RSS came to know that the regular mode of function they are undertaking else where in India is not enough to get a grip in Kerala society. The history of renaissance of Kerala had produced a new ethos of humanism, secularism and democracy. These values stood as a stumbling block in the way of RSS. CPI(M) in Kerala is the major force championing these values. This made them to think of a strategy of planned eradication of that party. Precisely with this aim in their heart they started annihilating the cadres and leaders of the party.

This strategy was evident in the plan adopted by RSS in the field of beedi workers of Malabar. 'The Hindutwa Rashtreeya of

Kerala' by one of the Pracharak P. Narayanan describes this effort as follows:

> The Kerala government introduced a new beedi-cigar legislation to the companies running in Malabar. This law incorporated the beedi workers under the factory law in the most unrealistic way. The government was not ready for even a talk with the management. As a result, the Mangaluru Ganesh Beedi and Bharat Beedi stopped working in the state and were shifted to Mangalore. The local beedi factories were working as the training centers of CPI(M). As the wages in Karnataka was very low when compared to Kerala they shifted their factories to Karnataka, Then in order to support hundreds of RSS and Jansangh workers in these industries we gave birth to a collectivity by name Mahalaxmi Traders and started manufacturing beedies on contract basis.

This was a sinister plan envisaged by RSS to get the command of 12000 odd workers on their side. In those days when almost all the beedi workers were demanding the implementation of Beedi-Cigar Act of the Govt. of India, the RSS wanted not to get it implemented for their petty political reasons. The stand adopted by RSS was totally rejected by the workers as they could easily assume that Mahalaxmi was nothing but a binami of the erstwhile Ganesh beedi.

A series of agitations took place on this front from December 1968. The beedi workers of Malabar agitated in front of the company head quarters of Ganesh beedi at Mangaluru and its branches in north Kerala. Then the RSS goons were there to help management in its anti labour activities throughout these depots. A protracted struggle was fought with the management of Ganesh beedi and the RSS goons on one side and the workers under the leadership of Communist Party on the other. This struggle was very intense in Thalasseri, Dharmadom, Thalayi and Kannur.

The company under the insistence of RSS tried to conduct the business under new labels such as Gurukripa and Mahalaxmi. It is at this juncture the Govt. headed by CPI(M) decided to organize a co-operative movement to solve the impending issue of unemployment among the beedi workers once for all and thus there emerged the historic Dinesh Beedi Company. Since then these companies became the target of the attacks. While looking back the history of the anti people activity of RSS, one can learn of the various methods adopted by them to put down the might of the communists. Local conflicts and differences of opinion are invariably seen in every society and it has its own way of redressal too. In these local conflicts, only beatings with bare hands were usually seen. But since the coming of RSS to the scene all these conventions were toppled in a planned way. It is the RSS goons who introduced the Danda for the first time in local confrontations. Later they introduced a 'S' shaped knife also in their attacks. In those days the RSS sympathizers engaged in a whispering campaign among the people that RSS is a trained and invincible force. It is also propagated that the trained RSS cadres are super human being having the courage of facing even a mass with their training and Dandas. In short, the RSS drill in open was a technique adopted by them to enforce a feeling of terror about them among the masses.

Dharmadom Panchayat also was a place of conflict between the beedi workers and RSS goons. It is now propagated through the RSS media that the violent conflicts between CPI(M) and RSS started in 1969 with the killing of Mr. Ramakrishnan who belonged to RSS. While going through the history of this conflict one can understand that the death of Ramakrishnan an RSS activist in 1969 was an accidental one that took place in an ordinary conflict between the two fractions at Vadikkal, Thalassery. In the initial stage of this conflict there was no intentional murder by either side except ordinary conflicts now and then. Just before the death of Ramakrishnan there was a conflict between SFI and RSS at

Chettitheruvu, the suburb of Thalassery. Com. Kodiyeri Balakrishnan, the Polit Bureau Member of the Party now, was a student activist then. He was also attacked by the RSS and was injured. In sequel to this confrontation, the RSS goons came in a group with their infamous Dandas and the masses of that area dared to confront this attack for the first time. As the RSS could not win over the situation despite their Dandas, much talked about training, and the heroic legends propagated, they made a retreat before the massive resistance. Ramakrishnan was fatally wounded in this confrontation and later succumbed to his injuries in the hospital. Citing this incidents the media always try to portray the CPI(M) as the murderers. But the reality is otherwise. Actually Ramakrishnan died in a confrontation purposely organized by the RSS goons. Astonishingly enough, there prevailed perfect peace just after the death of Ramakrishnan. Their trainings was of no use before a massive resistance and they tried to adopt various other forms of attacks in their effort to annihilate CPI(M) cadres. Their entire effort was concentrated in mobilizing a communal riot in Thalassery. Their first effort in this regard was actually made in 1954 at Naduvattom in Kozhikodu District. But in that riot RSS had only a complimentary role. But Thalassery riot of 1971 was the first of its sort conducted by RSS in Kerala.

Thalassery Riot

As stated earlier, it is a known strategy of RSS that whenever they want to have their grip in some place the first thing they would do is to ignite a communal riot there. A communal riot will clearly lay a line of demarcation between rival communities, the major one being the Hindu community. RSS will enter there as the champion struggling for the cause of the major communities. In this sense, communal riot becomes a route for the entry of RSS in a given political milieu. We may think why the RSS selected Thalassery as a place of entry through a communal riot. Two factors might have contributed to their ambitions. One is the presence of a large community of Muslims. Secondly, the predominance of CPI(M) was a major factor of attraction. RSS thought that in the event of a Communal riot they can be destroy two of their enemies; one being the Muslim minority community and the other CPI(M).

The riot broke out on 28th December 1971 and it lasted for one week with all its atrocities. There was a concerted effort for looting the shops of the minority community as well as demolishing their places of worship. On one occasion when the local mosque was under the threat of demolition Com. U.K.Kunhiraman of Local Committee of Mangattidam tried to block it and he was assassinated on the scene. He was the first martyr belonging to the CPI(M) activists in that riot. According to the police document altogether 569 violent incidents took place during that period in and around Thalassery. To be precise, Thalassery recorded 334 cases. In Chokly it was 47 cases, in Koothuparambu 51 cases, in Panoor 62 cases, in Edakkad 12 cases, in Kannur 1 case, in Mattannur 3 cases and in Dharmadam 59 cases were recorded. Around 247 Muslim households were attacked and looted, 147 of their shops ransacked. More than 63 mosques were attacked and countless vehicles of Muslim community were destructed. As far as Hindus are concerned 72 shops were ransacked, 4 houses looted.

Just after the riot was over, the government appointed Justice Joseph Vithayathil Commission to enquire about it on 14th February 1972. The Commission conducted their enquiry for 3 months and submitted its report on 31st May 1972. Altogether 70 persons represented various institutions and otherwise. Among the political parties that gave testimony to the Commission include Muslim League, Socialist Party, Bharateeya Jan Sangh, CPI, RSP, Organizational Congress, Ruling Congress, Communist Unity Centre and RSS. CPI(M) boycotted the Commission because even before the Commission started its function all other parties had alleged that the CPI(M) was behind the riot. Moreover the government had omitted the major party CPI(M) while a committee for assessing the total loss in the riot was formed. This too was a reason for the boycott. It is interesting to note here the statement given by Bharateeya Jan Sangh before the Commission.

> "The riot started with an attack conducted by Hindus on December 28. The immediate reason that provoked the Hindus to start attacking Muslims was political. As everybody knows CPI(M) was the party behind allowing the Malappuram District. It is in order to appease the sentiments of the Muslims that the CPI(M) allowed the formation of Malappuram District. But later the Muslim League turned against the CPI(M) and joined hands with Congress provoking the rivalry of the CPI(M) on this account. In order to settle their scores with Muslim League they instigated their Hindu supporters to attack Muslims of Thalassery."

This statement from the side of the Jan Sangh was intended to draw a further demarcating line between CPI(M) and Muslim community of Thalassery. Astonishingly enough the leaders of Muslim League also joined the band wagon of the RSS. But the mass at large of Thalassery believed that without the intervention of CPI(M) in the riot, Thalaserry would have turned to another Bheewandi, Meerut or Bombay. But the Commission was impartial to come to the following conclusions:

1. The various measures adopted by the Muslim League with the support of state power had created an antagonistic attitude among Hindus towards Muslim community. Hindus of Thalassery are of opinion that they won't get justice especially when the home portfolio was in the hands of Muslim League.

2. Evaluating the course of the riot it can be assumed that it is a planned one. The procession with the pot to Meloottu Madappura of Thalassery which was a ritual of Hindus was really planned to ignite violence. Ordinarily this procession used to take its route

through Town Hall Road. But this time the route is deviated and it was channeled through OV Road to undertake a long route that comes to 3 miles. More than that there were no children or women in the procession.

3. The malicious propaganda that a foot wear was thrown towards this procession from Noorjahan Hotel owned by a Muslim was a concocted one.

The real technique and style adopted by the RSS to conduct riot and provocation is elaborated in a book titled 'Is RSS Behind the Communal Riots' written by Subhadra Joshi, a well known and reputed Congress leader committed to the cause of secularism as follows:

> "The RSS used to propagate that Muslims are anti national to flair up the parochial sentiments of the majority community. Later they will instill a fear psychosis insecurity among the majority community. RSS people have the know-how to sneaking in the field of police and army and to create divisions there. They are also vigilant to give armed training among the youth of the majority community. Above all, they are good in propagating lies to draw communal divide in a society."

RSS was adopting the very same technique in Thalasseri as Subhadra Joshi elaborated in her book. Vithayathil Commission found out that RSS was inducting anti Muslim sentiments among the Hindus of Thalassery which in turn paved the way for a riot. Bharateeya Jan Sangh was also actively doing it, the Commission said.

In 1927 hardly after two years of the formation of RSS they organized a riot in Nagpur. In order to legitimize their intention they spread a lie that the Muslims threw chappals to the house of Dr. Hedgewar. They took out a procession against this through the town. Later they alleged that Muslim goons attacked this procession too. This propaganda gave a convenient situation for RSS to unleash a riot. In that riot the entire Muslim trading community was ruthlessly looted and a lot of Muslims were killed.

The methods adopted by RSS too are self telling. From the outset they decide which area is to be taken under the fold of the riot. Then they collect each and every details of that area. If the organizations under their command is incapable of collecting the information they form new local organization that are capable of doing it. When all these preparatory works are over, they start the riot to meet their ends. This method was adopted in Thalasseri too with all its details.

As already stated above the CPI(M) didn't give any evidence to the Commission. Yet in paragraph no. 220 of Justice Vithayathil Commission Report, it is stated that the CPI(M) took the lead to protect the Muslim community at the time of the riot. It was also stated that the CPI(M) was never a part of the riot. The party was least involved in it. At the same time on the very next day of the beginning of the riot CPI(M) came forward requesting the people not to get panic and not to get involved in the riot. This fact also was there in the Commission Report and the report extolled the role played by the beedi workers in the riot.

In those days of the riots the district committee of the CPI(M) came out with a general call to the people to take a stand against the riot. Accordingly a group of people headed by Pinarayi Vijayan, the then MLA of Koothuparamba, travelled from one place to another appealing not to take part in the riot. They dared to undertake this venture of the Party even in the areas where armed goons were getting ready for riots. In those tumultuous days I remember that I was also there in a group headed by Pattiam Rajan and K.V.Vasu travelling through various places appealing peace and communal harmony.

While the riot was broken out in Thalasseri the then Home Minister K.Karunakaran took a dubious stand of allowing the RSS goons to stage all their mischievousness. He thought the cultural dominance of the Communist Party in and around Thalasseri can be curbed using the situation of the riot. In the beginning of the riots the police force of the area was not full alert to face it. Moreover the Home Minister took a trip to Gujarat immediately after the riot took place. CPI(M) was the only party that appealed to the people to stay firm against the riot and to avoid bloodshed and killing. They released a statement as follows:

> "The communal riot in Thalasseri is spreading to nearby areas. Though Thalasseri is coming back to normalcy the violence and looting in the interior places are still there. A lot of Muslim women and children turned orphans. The government is not in full alert to face the communal riot. We appeal to all the people of Thalasseri to be in guard against communal violence and against the activities of RSS goons aimed at dismantling the strength of secularism and democracy. We appeal all to get united to reinstate the communal harmony and to isolate those who are trying to wreck it."

The media at large were also abusing the Communists in the days of riots. They presented the news in such a way that the people would think that the CPI(M) was a part of the riot and tried to get political mileage crushing their political enemies. This stand of the Government and the media, in essence gave reinforced vigor among the RSS goons in undertaking anti people activities. But the local people of that area were convinced out of their experience that CPI(M) was the only party to stand along with them in their plight for communal harmony, peace, democracy and secularism.

The RSS very soon understood that the communal riot of 1971 did not bring any advantage to them to get in to the political milieu of Kerala. More over they were isolated than ever before after the riots in Thalasseri. RSS has a well defined propaganda about the minorities as well as about the communists. Once Hegdewar said,

> "Hindus and Buddhists are seen only in Asia. The lion share of Hindus are in India. In this country we Hindus are 35 crores. The rest 10 crores are no more Hindus now. But once they were Hindus. But we lost them for ever because of our lethargy. Kashmir was supposed to be the beautiful garden of India. It is a matter of anxiety to me now that the Kashmir is predo-minated by Muslims now."

This is precisely the misguiding propaganda the RSS is undertaking about all national minorities of India. Now, coming to Communists RSS has their own versions. H.V.Sheshadri in his book 'Practicing the Concepts of RSS' says "The Communism as preached by various Communists is a theory against our national integration and culture." M.S.Golwalker says that the concept socialism doesn't have a bearing with our land. He is of opinion that socialism is anti nature both politically and psychologically.

RSS on Christian Minority of Kerala and the Nilakkal Issue

Nilakkal is a small village near to the renowned Sabarimala Temple. In 1983 when the earth work of State Farming Corporation was being done a cross made of stone was found out. The Christians of that area claimed that it is a cross established by St.Thomas 2000 years back and they began worshipping the cross. There is a Hindu temple nearby. While the Christians began worshipping the cross put up in a public land RSS tried to organize Hindus against this. An immanent threat of a communal riot was there in the atmosphere for some time and the followers of Congress stood divided on both sides. The Congress government was at a loss to understand what to do then. Almost all the secular sections were against the intentions of the RSS then. In 1987 the Congress ministry in the state was changed and the government under the leadership late E.K.Nayanar came to power. It is out of the consistent effort of this ministry that issue which would have taken the form of a communal riot was amicably settled. The approach of the RSS towards the nuns of Missionaries of Charity headed by Mother Theresa was also not different. On September 15, 2004 these nuns were brutally attacked by RSS-BJP goons.

The Babri Masjid incident in 1993 was of much significance in Indian politics. While the leaders of RSS were demolishing the church their cadres were ruthlessly engaged in killing the people of minority community throughout India. Though Kerala was the least affected state 10 persons were killed on that account. This ten death toll includes six Muslims and four Hindus. The RSS in this State then claimed that they could kill two more Muslims because of their inherent might. I still remember that in those days RSS brought out an enquiry report on Babri Masjid demolition in which they claimed that the "solar eclipse is over and Ajodhya is more bright now."

Poonthura Riot

Poonthura is a village in the suburb of Thiruvananthapuram, the capital city of Kerala. The northern part of this suburb is predominated by Muslim inhabitants. This place was quite known for its communal harmony up to 1992 when there flared up a riot between Hindus and Muslims. The RSS cadres started playing Kabady at Manjadikunnu of Poonthura. While they were playing they tried to provoke the local Muslims. That resulted in a riot. A Commission under the auspice of Aravindaksha Menon was appointed to enquire it. The Commission was of opinion that if the game spot of RSS had been shifted to the southern part of Manjadikunnu in the beginning itself the riot would not have happened. In Poonthura riot, besides RSS Islamic fundamental groups like ISS had also participated. It is usual when RSS start functioning in a place naturally the religious minority of the area will be scared. As an aftermath fundamentalist groups like ISS will also emerge there as a counterpart of RSS. In Poonthura apart from RSS (,) Jamayat-e-Islami was also there on the side of the Muslims. Astonishingly the Muslim League which was a partner of the coalition government was also there indirectly involved in the riot. Abdul Nasser Ma-adani of ISS is a fire brand orator of Islamic theology. He conducted a meeting at Poonthura days before the riot which also played a crucial role in instigating religious violence among the masses. All these factors ended in a riot in Poonthura. The Commission enquired the prose and corns of the riot. They were of the opinion that the attitude of the police was quite lethargic that it could not contain this violence in time. It was also found out that the DGP of the state left the state just two days before the riot. It may be remembered here that UDF leader K.Karunakaran the then Home Minister at the time of Thalasseri riot was not present in the state. Thus the UDF government's inefficient approach during communal riots was again proved Poonthura riot.

The Marad Riot

Marad is a costal area near Kozhikodu. Both Muslim fishermen and Hindu fishermen lived and were living a calm and harmonious life as in any other part in Kerala. As mentioned earlier the RSS got into the Hindu fishermen community there providing them paltry aids just like country made boat and fishing net. The Hindu fishermen known as Arayas are still backward when compared to the general progress attained by other sections of the people in Kerala. The Muslim fishermen of Marad are associated with either Muslim League or NDF, a fundamentalist outfit of fanatic Muslims.

The Marad riot was the ruthless one Kerala has ever witnessed. In the year 2002-03 alone 14 persons were killed there due to this riot. Sometimes this figure might be the largest one ever killed in a riot in Kerala. Taking into consideration of the tiny size of Marad which is just one kilometer in length and 500 meters in width this death toll becomes still alarming. It all started from an incident on the eve of New Year celebration where it is alleged a Muslim girl was abused. Immediately a riot broke out and four men, two each from either side were killed. On the 1st of January 2003 there was a conciliation talk between the leadership of Muslim League and BJP in the presence of the City Commissioner of Police. It is resolved in that meeting that no more killing should be taken place and no more provocation should be done by either side. But violating this agreement on the very next morning RSS goons attacked and killed an NDF activist in broad day light where the policemen were onlookers. In retaliation to this incident on May 3rd the NDF people conducted an armed insurrection against the Hindus killing 9 persons on the spot. This incident ignited a riot crossing all limits and Muslim community of the area were forced to flee from the area. The RSS was demanding a CBI enquiry in the riot. But the UDF government of that time was reluctant to leave the enquiry to CBI. It was alleged that Muslim League, a partner in the UDF regime had a hand in glove in this riot so the UDF was reluctant to conduct a CBI enquiry.

After the riot three relief camps were working in Marad. One was by Araya Samajam directed by RSS solely to give help to the Hindus. The second one was organized by Mahal Committee of Muslims. The third one was under the leadership of CPI(M) which was giving assistance to all without looking their religion. The government had a specific project of assistance which was divided to the first two sections. The UDF Government was not even helping the CPI(M) camp because of their petty political feud.

All these riots took place while UDF was in power and that too was the result of the appeasement of the UDF towards communal forces. Under the regime of UDF the government failed to file even the charge sheet in the case in time. More over the government allowed those who are in the forefront of the riot to give leadership to the peace movement too. The then government didn't take any interest to look into the intelligence forecast about the possibility of riots in that area both from Kerala and Tamilnadu intelligence. All these callous attitudes of the government proved beyond any shadow of doubt that they were inefficient to put down the riots in time. Instead of supporting the general sentiments of the masses and their staunch belief on secularism and democracy the right wing government run by UDF was always running after the communal forces seeking unholy agreements which later proved to be futile. History has once again proved that the communists and democratic forces of the state is the only reliable alley to the people to face the communal riots that affect Kerala now and then.

Chapter 3

The dubious role of RSS and Sangh Pariwar in Kerala Politics

The activities of RSS among Malayalees, started during 1940s were consistent in nature and cunning in its approach. Their sole aim was to get into the textural meaning of Malayalee sentiments and to build hegemony among them and to get electoral victories. The activities of RSS for the last seven decades in Kerala is a wonder that despite their influence here and there they could not even send a member in the legislature assembly so far. Generally speaking, the hold of RSS in the southern states of India is feeble compared to their growth in north and central India. Their frantic effort for the last three decades could not help them to fulfill their dreams of an electoral victory to the legislature assembly. They adopted almost all possible means that are quite unethical in its nature but in vain. This defeat has all the more infuriated the leaders of BJP and disillusioned the hopes of the cadres of Sangh Pariwar. The maximum they could attain in Kerala is limited to some local victories in certain local bodies. Earlier the leadership of BJP and RSS had a dream of producing at least one MLA and that dream itself is shattered now by the failure of various techniques adopted by them at different periods of time. RSS was a late comer generally to the southern states of India. Yet, as far as we know, the RSS could find out their own MLAs in other states except in Kerala. Now it is precisely this issue that haunts the sleepless nights of both the central leadership of RSS in Nagpur and BJP in Delhi. Kerala hitherto is a stumbling block in the South to the dreams of the Sangh Pariwar. Here I may depict the various theoretical methods adopted by RSS in their efforts to touch the general sentiments of Malayalees for the last six decades of their emergence.

We may start this analysis with the objective realities of 1950s in our state when RSS started its concerted efforts to get into the general polity of Kerala. As all of us know and as stated earlier, Kerala had its own typical way of social development. We are proud that we could attain complete literacy which is a unique phenomenon when compared to other states of India.

Surely the Left forces in Kerala in general and the Communist Party in particular contributed to this progress substantially. Almost all the trade union movements that started in Kerala in the beginning of last century had its own wing of literacy campaign. But even before this campaign started, the renaissance movement of Kerala had adopted the literacy campaign as the kernel of their activity. Before the emergence of the social renaissance in Kerala our state was a primitive one having all source of caste divide. The renaissance movement gave rise to a modern humanitarian ideology of equality and the various castes got united under their own social formations. For the Brahmins they had their Yogakshema Sabha inclusive of all the sub castes among the Brahmins. That is the case with the Nair Service Society as well as Sree Narayana Dharma Paripalana Sangham. In short, the renaissance movement brought in a new social identity to those sections of people chained in the sub castes bondage. This new identity was the objective reality of 1950s in Kerala.

No wonder that RSS tried to win over the social formations of Brahmins, Nairs and Ezhavas to cherish their dreams.

With this agenda in heart RSS promulgated an idea of a broad Hindu unity by name Hindu Maha Mandalam. The great leader of NSS, Mannathu Padmanabhan was interested in this move of a broad unity among Hindus. He elaborated the Hindu Maha Mandalam as an organization to protect the interest of the Hindus in Kerala. Mannathu Padmanabhan was elected as the leader of the Mandalam, RSS thought that they could win over SNDP to join in this Mandalam. They believed that the alignment of both NSS and SNDP under the banner of the Mandalam will enable the polarization of Hindus in the state. The meeting of the Mandalam was conducted in Kollam from May 12-18, 1950. RSS under the leadership of P. Madhavan played a crucial role in organizing the meeting. Mr. Shyamaprasad Mukherji who later became the leader of Jan Sangh was invited to attend in the meeting but he didn't attend. But S.S.Apthe was deputed to conduct talks between various leaders of the Mandalam.

Later Deendayal Upadhyay, the foremost leader of Jan Sangh, took a travel to Kerala in the December of 1953. He conducted discussions with the leaders of the Mandalam. The first committee of Jan Sangh in Kerala was constituted under the leadership of Mannar Gopalan Nair on December 31, 1953. Next year there was an annual meeting of Jan Sangh in Mumbai in which R. Shankar, the leader of SNDP, was an observer. From these instances it is clear that the RSS could mobilize the support of both SNDP and NSS in their development. But the Kerala reality was a different one. As the struggle against caste system in Kerala was so profound RSS could not mislead the ordinary workers of NSS or SNDP for long. The general masses of Kerala could easily come to know that Jan Sangh is a part and parcel of the erstwhile RSS. So they didn't join the Mandalam.

The activities of the Mandalam soon came to a standstill. Later, the Mandalam itself was withered and one section of it accepted RSS leadership and the other section joined the ranks of Congress in Kerala. Before the formation of Kerala State in 1956, Jan Sangh took part in the election to the Malabar District Board and their candidates were defeated hopelessly. Hence their first attempt of becoming a popular force in Kerala and to win elections was completely rooted out. A Communist led government was elevated to power in 1957 in Kerala. The government under the leadership of E.M.S. Namboodiripad was an expression of the long cherished hopes of the suppressed sections of the state. That government initiated steps to land reforms as well as to introduce social justice in the field of education. The conservative sections in the state under the leadership of Congress, Muslim League, SNDP and NSS were campaigning against the government in the guise of deteriorating law and order. They demanded the immediate dismissal of the elected ministry by the Government in the centre. This struggle is known as 'vimochana samaram'. As a result of this massive squatting the elected government was dismissed in March 1959. The Jan Sangh and RSS were also there to precipitate the struggle against the Communists and they could contribute some violent episodes in this counter revolutionary struggle.

The next was general election in Kerala was held in 1960. Com. EMS was contesting this election from Pattambi assembly constituency. Mr. P. Madhava Menon was the candidate of Jan Sangh. RSS agreed to withdraw P.Madhava Menon as anti communist votes might not be scattered. It shows that the RSS was in the habit of trading votes at the time of elections in favour of the right wing parties of Kerala right from 1960.This vote trading became very much rampant and unethical later. During the election of 1979 the Jan Sangh under the guise of Janata Party helped Congress in Kerala. BJP was formed in 1980 and in the 1982 elections they traded a majority votes in favour of Congress thereby reducing their polling to 2.7 percent while it was 4.5 percent earlier. The vote trading and the unholy alliance between the UDF and RSS in Kerala became more evident in a by-election to Lok Sabha in 1991. Mr. P.P.Mukundan who originally belonged to RSS was the state level organizational secretary of BJP. He was originally assigned the work of elections in Manjeswaram where the BJP thought that they can have a walk over there. Instead of going to Manjeswaram P.P.Mukundan camped at Kozhikode and had a detailed discussion with Mr. Kunhalikutty, the leader of Muslim

League. There was a formula emerged out of this discussion which is known as Vadakara-Baypore formula later. According to the formula UDF will present commonly agreed candidate to Vadakara Parliamentary constituency and in Baypore Assembly constituency. Adv. Ratna Singh who had close links with Mathrubhoomy, a leading Malayalam daily in Kerala stood as the commonly agreed candidate of both Congress and BJP. Dr. Madhavan Kutty who was the state President of Tapasya, the cultural wing of BJP, was the candidate in Baypore. Even the BJP leaders who were against this understanding for their own reasons could not block this understanding and formula. P.P.Mukundan was that much unquestionable with his support of RSS. This unholy alliance between Congress and BJP too could not bring the anticipated results. Both these candidates were defeated in that elections.

Actually the vote trading tactics adopted by the RSS leadership of the state was an optimum stage of their deterioration. Later many RSS and BJP leaders came out and disclose the vote trading practice of RSS in Kerala. Sri. K.Raman Pillai who was the state President of BJP in 1991 and later left to form his own party by name Janapaksham had exposed the deal to the maximum. Just after the deal was made open BJP appointed a commission consisting of Adv. Ayyappan Pillai, Dr. Xavier Paul and Palliyara Raman to go to the details of the allegation. The report of the commission was shocking. This Commission found that P.P.Mukundan was guilty in vote trading. After that the various groups within the BJP came in the open to meet their greedy interest of money making by trading votes at the time of elections.

On the basis of the report of the Commission the then president of the BJP, K.Raman Pillai approached the Sir Sangh Chalak at Nagpur through the Pranta Pracharak of Kerala. But despite all the evidences the RSS leadership was reluctant to take any action against P.P.Mukundan whereby making it amply clear that the central leadership of RSS was the real force of vote trading in Kerala. This practice of money making by the RSS was seen in the assembly elections of 2006. This time the trade contract was agreed between Kunhalikutty, General Secretary of Muslim League and O.Rajagopal, once a minister for state in the BJP ministry at the centre. Unfortunately on this occasion too the intension of Congress and BJP hadn't produce any result. In Kuttippuram Mr. Kunhalikutty who is considered as the stalwart of Muslim League was defeated by Dr. K.T.Jaleel, a low profiled leader in Malappuram District. The rank and file of the Muslim League of Kuttippuram could not digest the unholy agreement that Kunhalikutty had with the RSS.

In the Parliament election of 1999, 8.05% of the total votes went to BJP. But in 2001 it was reduced to 5.02%. This reduction is supposed to have happened out of the vote trading. It is then alleged that more than 60 assembly seats were in favour of UDF out of this adjustment. Mr. C.K.Padmanabhan, the leader of BJP while contesting the parliament seat in Thiruvananthapuram was hopelessly defeated by polling 4.84% of the total votes whereas when Mr. Rajagopal contested in the same seat earlier the polling percentage was 29.84. This vast difference in the polling percentage was a clear evidence of vote trading. The RSS and the followers of BJP had gone to the extent of attacking their own office at Trivandrum on this account. This state of affair has still depressed the leaders as well as cadres and now they have no alternative except indulging in frantic violence to assert their presence in the state. Before concluding I would like to mention here one of the statements of Adv. P.S.Sreedharan Pillai yet another state President of BJP. Mr. Pillai alleged that the Congress party in Kerala is the main beneficiary of the vote trading practice of RSS. In reply to his allegation Mr. Ramesh Chennithala, the President of Kerala Pradesh Congress Committee stated that the allegation is baseless. Then Mr. Pillai challenged the KPCC President with these words: "I am ready to make open the names of Congress leaders who approached me for votes. I challenge Mr. Ramesh to dare to take action against them". The president of KPCC was -silent towards this challenge. Mr. K. Karunakaran while he had gone out of the Congress had an opinion that there was vote trading in between Congress and RSS every time. Mr. K. Sudarsan, Sir Sangh Chalak of RSS has also revealed that during the assembly elections in 2001 Mr. Vayalar Ravi now a minister in Congress cabinet had met him at Nagpur seeking his support to the victory of Congress candidates in Kerala. Mr. Sudarsan had gone to the extent of saying the RSS was behind the victory of Congress in 2001.

Now the RSS camp in Kerala is a divided house with internal groups frantically accumulating wealth through unholy means. Mr. P.P. Mukundan is considered to be a veteran of this dubious game. RSS is always claiming it to be nationalist and always abusing others, especially minority communities, as anti nationals,. Recently it was exposed by rival groups that P.P.Mukundan is having alliance with the dreaded Mafia king Davood Ibrahim. Dawood Ibrahim is spending enormous funds to RSS in Kerala. This shocking statement is made by O.Rajagopal. But the hands of Rajagopal too is not clean says K.Raman Pillai of the Janapaksham Party. He revealed the corrupt practice of Rajagopal in allotting petrol pumps at the time of BJP ruling. In short both RSS and BJP in Kerala cannot claim to be nationalist and at the same time completely immersed in the quagmire of corruption. The immediate result of this deterioration is the down fall of cadres in RSS and their Shakhas in the state. This unprecedented down fall virtually shocked the leadership of RSS in Nagpur. It is in order to get out of this shocking situation RSS is adhering to their old practice of ruthless violence once again in this state.

Chapter 4

Party Villages

Even its political opponents will accept that the largest single party of Kannur District is undoubtedly CPI(M). The party has got a lot of influential villages in this district where members to Panchayat are elected unopposed. The mainstream media of Kerala always indulge in a concerted propaganda that CPI(M) is not allowing any other parties in their areas of influence and because of this authoritarian attitude they could keep their party villages under their control. It is so abused in the press that CPI(M) with the help of their domination in these villages is rigging the elections and not allowing the political opponents even to enter the polling booth. Their victory in various panchayats and even in Assembly constituencies are organized out of this undemocratic attitude. While comparing the vast areas of influence of the CPI(M) these propaganda may seem to be true. But it is otherwise when one looks into the reality and the relationship of the party with the masses of these localities.

The mainstream media always present the RSS in Kannur as a force opposing the authoritarian attitude of the CPI(M) and hence a democratic one. It is true that hundreds of villages are there where CPI(M) is an unchallengeable party in Kannur. It is this reality that made the media to abuse the Party as an autocratic one. In order to reveal the reality of this influence I would like to compare two different places where CPI(M) is a major force and RSS is having dominance. As stated earlier CPI(M) is the popular party having a lot of areas of influence. Though RSS was a smaller one in size in the district they also have a modicum of influential pockets of their own. One among them is Konkachy of Pattiam Panchayat. The 14th and 15th wards of this Panchayat is in Konkachi. RSS maintains its domination there for the last three decades. Konkachi is a remote place and quite backward both culturally and literally. Because of its isolation Konkachi is a spring board for illicit liquor and criminal activities. The old Praja Socialist Party was the major political force in that area before the emergence of RSS. As I explained earlier the Praja Socialist Party had allowed the RSS to grow there for their own reasons. This area is notorious for its criminal practices and even police or excise forces are not dare enough to conduct raids there. Instances are there where these forces are attacked in Konkachi by the anti social elements when they conduct routine raids. Hence Konkachi with its backwardness was quite convenient to be a hide out as far as the RSS is concerned.

After attaining the domination there in Konkachi the RSS turned that place a den of their hide out. The RSS criminals conducting violent conflicts in various parts of the district were given safe shelter in that area. Moreover the RSS used this base as a place to manufacture country bombs that are used in various actions both in the district and outside. The RSS goons made the place their den and all the activities going on there were according to their will and wish. The people are not daring enough to challenge them. Hence many who liked a decent life have flown from there and the rest are under the fascist claws living a suppressed life.

Because of the backwardness of Konkachi the land value in

that areas is astonishingly low. The land value in the nearby villages such as East Kadirur and Pattiam is Rs. 20,000 per cent. It is mere Rs.3000 in Konkachi. Konkachi is really a closed system from where no news is coming out. Once two journalists out of their curiosity had gone there to have a study on the function of RSS. It was with due permission of a district level leader of the RSS they had gone there. They had a chat with a local leader of RSS in Konkachi along with a photo session. When the news of the arrival of the journalist was spread, the local RSS armed goons entered the scene threatening and encircling them. These two journalists begged for their freedom to go out of that place through the already mentioned district leader of RSS. Instances were not rare where RSS cadres engaged in bomb making were burned to death in accidents.

RSS is maintaining their strong hold over this area by terrorizing the people and threatening them of isolation. Once it so happened in a marriage function when embellishing of the stage was done with the saffron ribbons the bride doubted whether it was a meeting of BJP. Getting angry at this satirical comment of the bride which was quite unintentional the RSS of Konkachi decided to boycott the marriage function. They didn't even allow others to take part in it. The family was virtually isolated. This is just an example of the cultural attitude of RSS towards the people living in their strong hold. There is one more instance that shows the arrogance of RSS. It happened during the electionto the parliament. When Com.Satheedevi was elected from the Vadakara parliament constituency the nearby places were celebrating the victory with crackers. A little girl in Konkachy also exploded some crackers in her house. The RSS people could not tolerate the action of that girl. On that very night a group of RSS people went there and threatened and abused the girl. The RSS could not forgive the girl despite her brother was an RSS activist. Later her brother got angry with this incident and he approached the RSS leaders to talk about the incident. The RSS gang surrounded him with weapons and that young man tried to run away from the scene. On his rush back unfortunately he fell in to a well and died. Police took a case on accidental death. In essence it was a cruel and cold blooded murder.

In comparison to this experience I would like to present the social life of a party village by name Malapattom. All the members in this Panchayat hail from LDF and elected unopposed. Astonishingly the topography of Malapattom is very similar to that of Konkachi with its remoteness. Malapattom is located in the middle of Kannur district. It is virtually an island. It is said that once Malapattom was a cast Hindu village with a Brahmin domination. All other inhabitants of that area came over there as the slaves of these Brahmins. In the 15th century these people were used for building homes. During the 14th century some traders belonging Islam religion also settled in Malapattom. The Christian people in that island reached there very late during 1960s. Malapattom is surrounded by the rivers on three sides and it comes to 19.30 sq. kilometers in area. There are twelve wards and the total number of inhabitants come to ten thousand.

Malapattom had a heroic past of anti imperialist struggle. The freedom movement of the nation was familiar to that place from 1930. The peasant organization was very strong in that village. There was a series of anti imperialist and anti feudal struggles in that area since the freedom movement. There was a school named RGM School in the village which was started in the latter half of 19th century, Now it is one among the 24 schools recognized by the government of Kerala in the Malabar area. We cannot even imagine now that a reading room was opened there under the leadership of peasant organization in 1936. As there are no industries working in this village major share of the workforce is engaged in construction works. Many people are engaged in service sector and in government service also. This village has two primary health centers, one higher secondary school, one UP school and 4 LP schools. One can see many public reading rooms in this Panchayat. There was only nominal income generated through land tax. The main source of their income comes from the selling of sand collected from the rivers. Though they are not economically rich, the transport system and the electricity supply is comparatively improved in this Panchayat. Various cultural activities are there in almost every village. The literacy of this area is 98% and computer literacy comes to 23%. More than 96% of the inhabitants are having their own houses. Though CPI(M) is the major party here other parties are also working without any complaint of intimidation from the side of CPI(M). A high rate of secular harmony prevails in this village where the collectivity and participation of various sections of the people are seen in almost all cultural activities. The opponents of the CPI(M) says that Malapattom is a party village. But the statistical survey of the government reveals the social life as detailed above.

These are two examples one in Konkachi and the other in Malpattom that itself reveals the difference of two parties and two cultural attitudes. As we have seen the RSS of Konkachi, Ayithara, Thokkilangadi and Panoor are terrorizing the people and dividing them on communal lines to continue their domination, the CPI(M) is giving stress to the communal harmony, cultural and development activities of the people of their village. While the CPI(M) is accountable to the people in their village the RSS is an alien force from the cultural milieu of Malayalees. They are least interested in the socio-cultural and political progress of the people as their total approach is aimed at just to continue their domination through terrorizing the people. Culturally speaking the RSS is ignorant of the cultural height of Keralites. Now RSS is finding it very difficult to maintain their limited strong holds in Kannur district.

The difference of these two parties are not taken into account by the media by placing both of them on the same plank. The media can conduct a study on their own about the different strong holds of both CPI(M) and RSS and can see the difference in the real social life in these different areas. Then I hope they can feel the difference of the two different approaches one standing along with history and the other negating the values of history.

Chapter 5

Upholding the Right for Resistance

It may be made clear here that CPI(M) is not the kind of a party which instigate violence against political opponents. CPI(M) believes that each and every party has got its own right to exist and work among the people. Moreover CPI(M) never advocate violence in their political activities. Yet the CPI(M) in Kannur has to engage in the violent clashes with RSS. How our party can explain the situation to the public. We are of firm opinion that CPI(M) never opted for violence in the beginning nor did it indulge in violence as it is a massive party in Kerala. Being the largest single party in Kerala the accountability of CPI(M) to the people of Kerala is very high. Naturally the party cannot indulge in irresponsible outbursts with its strong links and accountability with the people. But the state of affair of RSS is otherwise. They are a negligible force restricted to certain pockets of Kannur district. Being a minor section they can adopt any sort of practice without any accountability. As the RSS doesn't have any class organizations under them they are virtually unanswerable for their activities to the people. Instances will show that after a series of attacks from the side of the RSS the CPI(M) in Kannur district is forced to retaliate it in the same coin. Here I may state that the CPI(M) has high esteem on the approach of Gandhiji on violence and non-violence. It may be remembered that Gandhiji has commented on the issue very may times. I may quote Gandhiji here:

> "If I were living in a forest as a farmer I will be constrained to resort to violence even in a small level. There I may be compelled to eradicate monkeys and birds that may come to eat out the crops. I can adopt such a method in that situation on my conviction that destroying crops is a sin. As far as I am concerned evil and virtue in a society is rather a relative one. A virtue in a given situation may be otherwise in a different situation."

Gandhiji has also opined that some one who is fleeing a village where a cheetah entered is a coward and one who dares to kill it is a courageous one. All the clashes in which CPI(M) was involved in Kannur district were done as counter attacks for self defense.

The fundamental rights of self defense is allowed to any individuals as well as to any party. The real spirit of the counter attacks for self defense cannot be simply equated with the planned attempts of murder. If CPI(M) had resorted to counter attacks against RSS it is because of the series of unruly attacks conducted by them. As stated earlier the media always failed to analysis the concrete situation of each and every clashes between CPI(M) and RSS. They always chant a slogan that CPI(M) is retaliating the RSS in the same coin and both sections are manufacturing bombs and using them everywhere. They alleged that both of them are equally responsible for the clashes. By making such a statement what the journalists lack is their basic responsibility to go to the minute details of each and every incidents as well as their failure to understand the difference of the accountability of the different parties involved.

The Muslim brothers of Thalasseri will never forget the immense atrocities committed by RSS in their houses. At the time of the communal riot of 1971 the RSS goons virtually ransacked their shops and houses and looted whatever valuables they had. Even now they know various people who had amassed immense wealth out of that riot and who are still having hotel business and transport business of their own. So in order to have an impartial assessment of a situation the journalists should gather their evidence from the victims for they may know everything better than anybody else.

RSS always consider the minority community as betrayers of our national independence and fifth columnists of national enemies. It is their ideological position that compels them to disbelieve or distrust the Muslim minority of India. Once somebody is identified as a betrayer it gives an ideological legitimization to annihilate them. Moreover that act of annihilation becomes a pious one in the background of a perverted national interest. As the RSS is always cherishing this idea of annihilation of enemies, their entire activities is reduced to chose of plane of killers. A party like CPI(M) cannot adopt these sorts of a lower level politics because of the responsibilities that various classes in the society have entrusted upon them. This is the basic difference of both these two parties which are open neglected by the fourth estate. RSS are really a group of people committed to put into practice the ideas promulgated by Dr. Hedgewar and Guruji Golwalker.

Jayakrishnan Master one of the RSS activists was killed in a class room in the day light in front of children. The media in Kerala made a big hue and cry over it. Five persons were convicted in that case for capital punishment. That murder was portrayed as a rare among the rarest incident of ruthless violence. But we cannot forget that it was not the first instance where a class teacher was killed in front of his students. Com. Raju Master, a CPI(M) activist and a school teacher, was put to death before his students on 26th October 1978. Com. P. Damodaran Master who was a Local Secretary of CPI(M) too was attacked before his students in 1972 where he later succumbed to his wounds. While these sorts of unilateral attacks were conducted one after the other naturally the people at the victim end will resort to counter attacks. In our experiences wherever the attackers are countered by peoples force there they had taken the due lessons of history.

Mr. P. Parameswaran who is known as Parameswarji among RSS people had once stated just after the conflicts in December 1999 that if the CPI(M) can avoid the ideological opposition against RSS peace will prevail everywhere. In this statement he is demanding a big price from the side of CPI(M) to stop their ideological offencive against fascism that communist party can never do. RSS had a dream once that they can become a massive force in Kerala and they considered Thalasseri Taluk as a place where they can fulfill their dream. Later they came to realize that the resistance from the side of CPI(M) is the real factor that shattered their dream of development.

In the first half of 2000 RSS had a leadership camp at Cherukolpuzha in the District Pathanamthitta where they adopted a four point programme as follows:

1. They resolved to double the strength of RSS in Kerala and to enhance the strength of BJP to three times. They requested the central leadership of RSS to provide funds and leadership service to attain this goal.

2. They appealed the central leadership to adopt the Kannur district to their direct control to enhance RSS work and also requested the leadership to chalk out various plans to operate more Shakhas and to imbibe more and more spirit to the cadres.

3. They have also resolved in that meeting to oppose the communist government in Kerala with all possible strength.

4. They gave shape to a new strategy of anti-Christian propaganda in Kerala as there is a vast section of Christians in Kerala. From these resolutions it becomes clear that RSS gives a special hust in their activity to Kannur district. They are really practicing a major design of violence specially conceived for this district. They are considering not only the CPI(M) people as their enemies here. Even Congress workers and workers of Janata Dal are also there who became praye to the cruelty of RSS goons.

I can earnestly say that nowhere in Kerala CPI(M) had taken any initiative of armed clashes against RSS. It is true that we are a party ideologically different and opposing to the fascist ideas of the RSS and Sangh Pariwar. That does not mean that we are to attack and kill them. Needless to say a massive party like CPI(M) which is answerable to the people cannot rely on such activities as armed clashes always. That doesn't mean we have not indulged in retaliation. We are not cowards as stated by Gandhiji who will sit idle against series of inhuman atrocities unleashed opponents. We consider the greatest thing in social life is the right of a peaceful living and allowing others also a peaceful life. When some sections of the society is ruthlessly indulging in the activities of shattering the peaceful life of the people, our party dares to face them in their own coin and to contain them for the sake of the people. It is our strong believe that if RSS was not retaliated as we did in Thalasseri that place would have turned to a Gujarat, Orissa or Madhya Pradesh.

We genuinely consider the social peace as a great dream of the people. We feel that the enemies of the people should be put down at the earliest and we consider that work as our social responsibility. As communists we dare to show the people the real path of progress.

Chapter 6

Infiltration Through Caste Organization

The RSS tried to enter in the forefront of the society by not only using religion as their weapon. However they also formed organizations for labours, farmers, business men, teachers, students etc. Though they had declared that they have no 'Ism' and are not interested in politics, it is at their instigation the Bharateeya Jan Sangh was formed in 1951. Again in 1980 the formation of BJP was also an execution of the policy decision of the RSS.

A conflict arose in the 1979 among the cadres as to whether one can be a member of Janata Party and RSS simultaneously? And eventually the RSS decided to form BJP including the all leaders and cadres of the old Jan Sangh. Philosophy upheld by the RSS is the cast system prevailed in ancient India. M.S.Golwalker observed the caste system in ancient India as distinctive and unique. When they realized that they can not effectively win over the people through caste system, they tried to reach them through the caste organizations.

Discrimination and evil practices in the name of caste was extremely high in Kerala. There arose many organizations during the period of renaissance to fight out the evil practices in Kerala. SNDP, NSS, Sadhu Jana Paripalana Yogam, Dheevara Sabha, Araya Samajam, Sahodara Prasthanam etc. are some among them.

These organizations encouraged the people to get rid of the religious conservatism. As RSS always stand for Hindu unity the caste divide in Hinduism is a hindrance for their goal of Hindu unity.

M.S.Golwalker had visited office of the Hindu Mandalam on 14th November 1952 and had a talk with R.Shankar and Mannathu Padmanabhan. Shyama Prasad Mukherji had also visited Kerala during this period. The awful conservatism of these leaders of Kerala led to the disintegration of Hindu Mandalam and the political party shaped by it. It also prevented the chance of RSS leaders to play a major role in this direction.

P.Parameshwaran, one of the eminent theoreticians of RSS has evaluated the situation in his observation that since the emergence of Shri Narayana Guru, the Kerala society has treaded a new path totally different from the old one. The immediate sequel to the social reformation of Kerala society was the formation of trade union and peasant organizations under the left and progressive parties.

Despite the draw back the RSS continued its reliance on caste organization for its development. Precisely with this idea in its heart the RSS gave birth to Hindu munnani in 1982. Hindu Munnani had a live relation with SNDP, NSS, Veera Shaiva Sabha, Vellala Mahasabha, Vilakkithala Nayar Samajam, Rashtra Dharma Parishat, Gowda Saraswat Sabha, Kerala Hindu Mission, Kerala Harijan Samajam, Peruvannan Sabha, Yoga Kshema Sabha, Vishwakarma Service Society, Young Men Hindu Association, Ayyappa Seva Sangham, Chinmaya Mission, Ramdas Mission etc.

Under the patronage of Hindu Munnani, BJP had faced the 8th Parliamentary election and state legislative assembly election in 1987. "Hindu Vote for those who uphold the interest of Hindus" was the slogan of Hindu Munnani. The six candidates who represented the Hindu Munnani had secured an average 2.15% of total votes. The BJP candidate had secured 20% i.e. 1,10,449 votes in Thiruvana-nthapuram parliamentary constituency and in the Ranni legislative constituency their candidate got 10% votes.

This result excited the Sangh Pariwar leadership. Hence in 1987 Hindu Munnani has placed 39 candidates in the legislative assembly election and except seven, all other candidates contested election with Lotus as their symbol. In that election UDF was defeated and LDF assumed power. Though BJP and Hindu Munnani had not got a single seat they secured 6.57% of total votes polled. In Thiruvananthapuram East constituency they got 27.96% votes.

This development motivated UDF and Sangh Pariwar to think in the same direction. They realized that LDF is getting benefit when they fight each other and this realization insisted them to unite in the legislative assembly election in 1991. Discussions were conducted in many levels. Mr.Kunhikannan an editor of 'Janmabhoomi' and RSS mouthpiece has commented these efforts in his book 'K.G.Marar, Rashtreeyathile Snehasagaram"

> "As the desire to win the election in 1991 became strong we decided to join hands with anyone to achieve this aim. Accordingly P.P.Mukundan, senior RSS Pracharak was appointed as secretary to chalk out the strategy. Two journalists played major role in this effort. Initially there was a doubt whether BJP and Muslim League would go together. The detailed discussions between BJP and Muslim League leaders convinced them that they could move together. It was agreed that Muslim League would vote for the candidate in Thiruvananthapuram and in turn BJP would help the UDF candidates in other constituencies."

Later a commission was appointed to enquire the practice of 'vote trading' in BJP. The commission raised the question, how the Sangh Pariwar cadres could vote to Muslim League as it is built on anti Muslim sentiments. As no ideological solution could be found out on this question, a lot of cadres became disillusioned and they left the party. Hence the tactics of associating the caste organization like NSS could provide some result in the beginning but it was a total failure in long run. The cadres could easily understand the irrationality of the leaders on this account. When BJP came to power in centre in 1998 they tried to tempt and warn the caste organizations to stay along with them.

Before the unification of Kerala in 1st November 1956 so many dissimilarity were there between the regions of Malabar and Travancore-Cochi. Malabar was part of Madras province in British India while Travancore-Cochi was a Princely State. Caste organizations had interfered in the social life and brought many changes in Travancore-Cochi but in Malabar they had no role in the development of social reforms.

Vellappalli Nateshan, general secretary of SNDP advocated an idea to bring out caste organizations in Malabar. This idea originated when BJP came to power in centre. This can be observed as a result of the ultimate aim of Sangh Pariwar to infiltrate in Kerala society through cast organizations. It was so argued by Mr.Nateshan that almost all the martyrs who laid their life in the development of Communist movement in Malabar belonged to backward castes. He was promulgating a theory of caste politics instead of class politics put forth by the communist party. CPIM was the only party who fought against the re-establishment of the caste oriented politics in Malabar where the people have a unity and political enlightenment above the narrow caste outlook. While anti-CPIM parties and leading media were encouraging to restore caste oriented politics CPIM had relentlessly fought against it.

Vellappalli Nateshan claimed that he was sending a flag ship to Kannur in the year 2003. He insisted that Thiyya community of Malabar which was a synonym to the Ezhava community in Travancore should be united on the plank of their caste. There is nothing wrong in proclaiming one's cast he said. He conducted a Malabar Mahasangamam on this plea. It could not arouse a big inspiration among the Thiyya community in Malabar but BJP was much enthusiastic in that Mahasangamam where people from five northern districts were participated. Almost all the leaders of BJP including P.P.Mukundan, P.K.Krishna Das, P.P.Karunakaran, O.K.Vasu and K.K.Balram of RSS were present in the meeting. This Mahasangamam was conducted at a time when the Jayalalita government in Tamilnadu introduced an anti-conversion law there. The BJP leadership was of the opinion that such a law should be promulgated in Kerala also. The BJP was against the formation of Malabar Dewosam Board and this demand was also raised by Mr.Vellappalli Nateshan. BJP thought the caste politics propounded by SNDP in Malabar will yield a positive response from the people. But that expectation proved to be futile.

Chapter 7

The Path Soaked with Blood

Gandhiji was assassinated on 30th January 1948 in Delhi. He was shot dead by one Nathuram Godse a Hindu fundamentalist. Was there any involvement of RSS in the killing of Gandhi ? Technically speaking we do not have any direct evidence about the involvement of RSS in the annihilation of Gandhiji. But as it was an unruly act of a Hindu fundamentalist and RSS being an ideological and political instrument of Hindu fundamentalism that organization had an indirect psychological involvement in that assassination. This is evident from a letter written by the then Home Minister Sri. Vallabhai Pattel who was known as the 'iron man' of India and was having a soft corner towards Hindu fundamentalism. This letter was addressed to late Dr. Syamaprasad Mukharjee written on 18th July 1948 in which Pattel had categorically stated that Hindu Maha Sabha was an active partner in the conspiracy of the killing of Gandhi and the activities of RSS was a major threat to the Government and the nation as a whole. Dr. Syamaprasad Mukharjee was the founder member of the Jan Sangh which was the fore runner of BJP. Pattel's criticism towards RSS was further more strong while he wrote a letter to the Sir Sangh Chalak of RSS on the 11th September 1948. In that letter he stated that the speeches of RSS leaders were quite venomous and this venom was an indirect cause that inspired Godse to shoot Gandhiji. Pattel even alleged in that letter that the RSS all over India celebrated the death of Gandhi and distributed sweets as a mark of their celebration while the entire world was weeping over it.

In my opinion, a close study of Gandhiji's assassination and the recent genocide in Gujarat will stand testimony to the violence of Hindu Fascism promulgated by RSS. While going through the post independent history of India one can understand the various communal riots in our country are not an imminent expression of the suppressed feelings of the people involved in it. They are all well planned and designed activities of the RSS. The various riots from 1960 to 1980 are all happened in different industrial centers of India. Curiously enough one can learn that riots have been taken place in industrial centers while some of the trade unions are getting stronger in industrial belts. Wherever the industrial growth and the trade unions go side by side, RSS targets those places for communal riots. The riots that took place in Kota in Rajasthan in the year 1989 is an ideal example of the pre-planning of RSS in this issue. When that riot took place, CITU was a major trade union force in that area. The perseverance among all the workers of that area above the Hindu-Muslim divide was intolerable to RSS. This was the immediate reason for that riot through which they aimed to re-establish the old Hindu-Muslim division once again in that area. RSS always try to divide the workers according to their religious belief while the progressive and democratic forces try to imbibe a historical class concept among workers. On contrary to it, RSS always tries to draw a communal line among the workers. In short, they divide the workers based on communal consideration. This is quite evident from the experiences of the communal riots in the major industrial centers. Whenever RSS finds a place which is economically and politically developed and predominantly inhabited by Muslims they start implementing their preplanned design of targeting that area for another communal riot. The best example for this design is the communal riots in Bihar Sharif of 1980. Going through the history of communal riots in India instigated by RSS one can see a major difference between the riots of pre Nineties and that of post Nineties. Both BJP and RSS changed their methods of conducting riots in the period after 1990. This shift in their approach was adopted according to the political deterioration of the Congress Party in India.

The decade commencing from 1990 witnessed the growth of BJP and the decline of Congress party in Indian politics. The general design of communal riot instigated by RSS in this decade was very much aimed at gaining political power. The controversy on Ayodhya and the demolition of Babri Mazjid enabled BJP to enhance their vote bank. It is after the demolition of the Mazjid the BJP became a predominant force in Indian politics. More over BJP could find out a tactical victory of their communal politics with this demolition. Since then BJP is adopting this tactics of communal divide all over India the latest being the Modiism of Gujarat. Now, it has attained the dimension of attacking various Christian churches in Orissa. RSS is having now their own agenda both in Tamilnadu and Kerala and is working on it.

The recent history of India is the history of development of democracy too. But the history viewed from the angle of BJP it is the history of communal riots. Here are some riots organized by RSS in the post independent India.

The Day Book of Communal Riots since 1947

There was a communal riots in Punjab mainly centered in both Lahore and Amritsar from march to August 1947. This riot started before independence and continued even after independence. This was directly a product of partition and Punjab was the worst hit states of India during the time of partition. Then armed bands of people pounced upon innocent Muslims killing 5000 people and leaving 3000 wounded. Astonishingly enough, the riot of 1947 has a lot of commonness with that of 2002 in Gujarat with its planning and implementation.

The Jabalpur Riot of 1961

As I have stated earlier RSS will always draw a line of divide between Muslims and Hindus in the trade union front. In Jabalpur which was a centre of Beedi industry, they worked this tactics out when son of a beedi worker belonging to Muslim community eloped with a girl belong to Hindu community. There was an enquiry commission with Justice Sivadayal Srivasthava was to enquire it. But this enquiry didn't reach anywhere.

The Rurkhela, Kolkotta, Jamshedpur Riot of 1964

This riot also took place in an industrial centre. This time the riot was broken out as a sequel to a rift between Hindu Muslim traders indulged in liquor business. RSS adopted a propaganda here that the Muslims were unduly getting a major profit in the business. Actually this riot was a retaliation of the attack from the side of the Muslims towards Hindu's in Bangladesh. More than 2000 Muslims were killed in this riot.

The Riot in Hathiya in Ranchi in August 1967

There was a movement mainly from the side of the Muslim students to get Urdu accepted as the second national language. They staged a massive rally for it and there was stone pelting in the rally which ignited a riot. More than 164 Muslims and 20 Hindus were killed in this riot. As usual there was an enquiry commission in this incident too which observed that RSS was involved in it.

The Riot of Aurangabad in 1968

Curiously enough this riot has a typical beginning. A Muslim boy chased out a cow that entered his shop. RSS took it as a convenient opportunity for a riot. It is to be noted here that the Aurangabad riot had an unfortunate participation of the congress party.

The Riot in Assam in March 1968

Here also a cow played the major role as a reason for a riot. A cow brought up by a Muslim had entered a settlement of a Hindu while chasing it out of the compound the cow got hurt. In retaliation to this a Hindu boy was beaten by Muslims and that evoked the riot. Altogether 41 Muslims and 41 Hindus were killed in the riot.

The Ahmadabad Riot of 1969

This riot was originated around the Jagannatha temple of Ahmadabad and spread to more than 25 places around. Altogether 512 persons were killed in it. There was an enquiry commission under Justice V. Jagan Mohan Reddy to enquire it and the commission found out the RSS also guilty in it. The congress party was not spared by the commission. In this incident the congress party went to the extent of calling the Muslims anti national.

The Riot of Bheewandi of Maharashtra in 1970

This riot was unique with its aggressive nature and death toll. Chatrapati Shivaji is a legendry figure in Maharashtra. There used to be a mammoth rally every year in commemoration of Shivaji. Both Muslims and Hindus used to take part in it. But in that festival in 1970 as the procession was going on there were slogans against Muslims in the rally. Immediately the rally turned violent killing 59 Muslims and 17 Hindus. Late Smt. Indira Gandhi came out in open against RSS on this issue. There was a commission headed by D.P. Madan to enquire the riot. This commission criticized RSS and the police for their partisan stand.

The Mahad riot in Maharashtra in 1970

This riot was actually a sequel to the Beewandi riot. The enquiry commission appointed for the investigation of Beewandi riot enquired about this riot also. RSS was abused by the commission as a force taking advantage out of the communal sentiments of the people.

The Day Book of Violence and Riots since 1970 in a Nutshell

Year of Riots	Place of Riots	Death Tall	No. of Injured
1970	Bhivandi	76	More than 200
1970 May	Gulgav	42	More than 100
1970 May	Mahad	Not available	18
1972 November	Nonari & Sajini in UP	Not available	Not available
1977 October	Varanasi in UP	5	About 100
1978 October	Aligarh in UP	Not availabe	Not Avilabe
1978 September	Hyderabad in AP	19	Above 100
1979 April	Jamshedpur in Bihar	120	1000
1980 August	Moradabad in UP	1500-2000	Above 10000
1981 April	Bihar Sherif in Bihar	80	200
1982 September	Meerut	Not availabe	Not available
1982 December	Baroda in Gurajt	17	50

1983 May	Maloor in Karnataka	Not available	Not available
1983 June	Malegav in Maharastra	Not available	Not available
1983 October	Hazaribad in Bihar	45	150
1984 May	Bhivandi in Maharastra	146	611
1985 April	Ahmedabad in Gujarat	300	More than 1000
1986 July	Ahmedabad in Gujarat	59	80
1987 April	Meerut,	81	40
1989 October	Indoor in MP	27	100
1989 September	Kota in Rajastan	Not available	Not Availble
1989 March	Bhadrak in Orissa	17	More than 100
1990 April-December	(During the period of Radhayatra)	224	275
1990 April	Kanpurin UP	30	100
1990 October	Ahmedabad in Gujarat	Not available	Not Available
1990 October	Jaipur in Rajastan	52	144
1990 October	Jodpur in Rajastan	Not available	Not available
1990 October	Lucknow in UP	Not available	Not available
1990 November	Agra in UP	31	69
1990 October	Delhi	100	1000
1990 October	Hailakandi in Assam	37	100
1990 October	Patna in Bihar	118	Above 1000

1990 November	Kanpur in UP	13	100
1990 December	Hassan & Mysore in Karnataka	Not available	Not available
1990 October	Hyderabad in AP	165	350
1990 Dec.	Hyderabad in AP	134	Above 1000
1991 January & April	Gujarat	38	170
1991 April	Baroda	Not available	NA
1991 May & November	Banaras in UP	Above 50	More than 100
1991 May	Baroda	28	100
1992 October	Seethamadi in Bihar	44	100
1992 December	Surat, Gujarat	200	About 1000
1992 December-93 January	Bombay	1000	More than 5000
1992 December	Bhopal	143	More than 500
1995 April	Chithradurga in Karnataka	Not available	Not available
1995 June	Rankhandi in UP	Not available	Not available
1995 July	Palmo in Bihar	4	50
1998 January	Kanpur in UP	Not available	Not available
1998 February	Ajmir	3	10
1998 May	Moradabad	3	50
1998 June	Hyderabad in AP	Not available	Not available
1998 July	Bardili in Gujarat	Not available	Not available

1998 October	Nalanda in Bihar	3	39
1998 October	Ahva in Gujarat	Not available	Not available
1998 December	Suratkal in Karnataka	12	100
1999 January	Manoharpur in Orissa	3	10
1999 Jauary	Ahmedabad in Gujarat	2	10
1999 July	Harda in MP	1	10
1999 December	Aurangabad in UP	Not available	Not available
1999 September	Surat in Gujarat	7	27
2000 December	Kolapur in Maharastra	Not available	Not available
2001 March	Nalanda in Bihar	8	6
2001 April	Beever in Rajastan	Not available	24
2001 June	Jamnar in Maharastra	Not available	Not available
2001 July	Moradabad in UP	6	10
2001 August	Amravani in Maharastra	2	30
2001 August	Ahmedabad in Gujarat	1	10
2002 January	Gujarat (Gujarat Riot)	2000	More than 10000
2002 February	Kethen in Hariyana	Not available	Not available
2002 March	Dhivani in Hariyana	Not available	Not available
2003 March	Gujarat	Not available	Not available
2003 January	Mungeer Town in Bihar	2	10

2003 March	Holly Celebration in UP	3	59
2003 April	Raj Gangpur in Orissa	2	47
2003 September	Baroda in Gujarat	1	75
2003 October	Agra in UP	1	10
2003 November	Veerang in Gujarat	3	45
2003 November	Pardani in Maharastra	Nil	35
2004 January	Jabuva in MP	1	10
2004 February	Vadodhara in Gujarat	3	13
2004 March	Ahmednagar in Maharastra	Not available	Not available
2004 June	Meerut in UP	2	20
2004 July	Peravel in Gujarat	2	8
2004 August	Parbani in Mharastra	Nil	23
2004 October	Badhoni in UP	Nil	49
2004 November	Silchar in Assam	Nil	Many injured
2005 February	Vadodhara in Gujarat	1	23
2005 February	Rajnand Gav in Chattisgrah	Not available	Not available
2005 February	Dhar in MP	Not available	Not available
2005 April	Dhilwada in MP	Nill	Many
2005 March	Faizabad in UP	6	10
2005 April	Mandal Town in Rajastan	Not available	Not available

2005 May	Bhivandi in Maharastra	Nill	Many
2005 Oct.	Maru in UP	14	100
2006 Feb	Muzhafar Nagar in UP	Not available	Not available
2006 March	Muzhafar Nagar	Not available	Not available
2006 April	Aligarh in UP	4	13
2006 April	Thane in Maharastra	Not available	Not available
2006 May	Vadodhara in Gujarat	4	12
2006 June	Prathapgut in UP	2	25
2006 Sept.	Uzamabad in Maharasta	Not available	Not available
2006 Oct.	Mangalore in Karnataka	2	10
2007 Dec.	Baliguda & Dulbani in Orissa	9	5000

Virtually in every month if not in every week, there is a communal clash in India where on one side either RSS or anyone of the Sangh Pariwar is there as the aggressive Hindu fascism. Those who knowingly or unknowingly contribute to the planned violence of these fascists are surely putting down the great Indian culture of communal harmony and democracy.